BRIDGE
TNT and COMPETIT

BRIDGE:

TNT and COMPETITIVE BIDDING

Dick Payne & Joe Amsbury

Batsford Bridge Series Editors:
Tony Sowter and Joe Amsbury

B T BATSFORD Ltd   London

ISBN 0 7134 25423 (cased)
ISBN 0 7134 25431 (limp)

Typeset by Probray Press Ltd

and printed in Great Britain by
Billing and Sons Ltd
London, Guildford and Worcester

for the publishers
B.T. Batsford Ltd
4 Fitzhardinge Street
London W1H OAH

Contents

Introduction

In an RAF billet on the Wiltshire Downs a regular solo whist school was doing National Service. One player repeatedly offered to teach the others to play bridge, which, he said, was a much better game than solo. One Saturday night when our morale was lower than usual, we didn't have the energy to refuse. We learnt to play bridge. When lights went out that night we took the table and cards out into the latrines to finish the rubber, and from that time we never played solo again.

Each person developed his own ideas about bidding, and arguments were dogmatic and vociferous. In the midst on one of the noisier arguments, Taffy, who was not counted as much of an artist at the game, let fall the portentous words, 'But it says in my book that...' The effect was electric, there was a stunned silence while everyone grappled with the import of this remark. That people actually wrote books about bridge, and that Taffy, Taffy of all people, had read one. In the course of the next few sessions Taffy remained unperturbed by jocular references to 'his book', in fact he revelled in the notoriety it conferred on him, and it soon became apparent that everybody else would have to read Taffy's book just to see if he had got it right.

Some weeks later Taffy produced a bridge problem from a national newspaper; he called it a double dummy problem, and he said he couldn't do it. The fact that Taffy couldn't solve the problem did not in itself occasion much surprise, but there was great merriment when it transpired that all four hands were on view and Taffy still couldn't do it. Taffy's indignant retort was, 'Well you do it then'. Amidst such airy assurances as 'I'll do it', and 'That shouldn't take long', the brains of the billet went to work. An hour later Taffy was triumphant, nobody else could do it. From that moment anything in print about bridge was eagerly devoured and passed on.

Bridge has never ceased to fascinate me, and I have continued to read voraciously about the game. In the course of such reading I came across Bridge Moderne de la Defense by Jean Rene Vernes, where the theory of total number of tricks is put forward. Why should some deals produce no more than a part score, whereas others yield a game, or even a slam, in either direction? What governs the total number of tricks, and is this TNT predictable in the bidding? These questions are of vital importance to all bridge players, and the answers have far-reaching consequences which affect the whole structure of competitive bidding.

PART I
TNT

Chapter 1
Fit in a Competitive Auction

'Fit' is a term used loosely to describe three different concepts. Most constructive bidding sequences are designed initially to discover the existence of an eight card trump fit, and players know that a 4-4 trump fit will sometimes produce a trick more than a 5-3 trump fit.

'Fit' is also used to denote the possession of an honour card in partner's side suit. Trial bids and splinter bids aim at discovering whether partner's honour cards are well placed; if they are, the hands are said to fit well.

Perfect 'fit' implies all honour cards working at maximum efficiency with no minor honours being wasted, a long trump suit, and singletons and voids facing potential losers. High contracts can be made on a low point count with perfect fit.

♠ K97	N	♠ AQ65
♥ A862	W E	♥ 753
♦ 764		♦ 1053
♣ AQ9	S	♣ KJ6

A sound minimum opening bid faces a completely average hand. There is no trump fit, and a contract of 1♥, 1♠, or 1NT might be fulfilled with an overtrick.

A dramatic transformation is achieved by giving one hand some distributional features:

♠ K98742	N	♠ AQ65
♥ A8	W E	♥ 753
♦ —		♦ 1053
♣ AQ942	S	♣ KJ6

Exactly the same high cards are present, but now there is a perfect fit in two suits and the grand slam in spades is a near certainty.

Changing the suits around removes the perfect fit:

♠ K98742	N	♠ 1053
♥ A8	W E	♥ KJ6
♦ —		♦ AQ65
♣ AQ942	S	♣ 753

There is still an adequate fit in spades, but with the wasted duplication in the diamond suit declarer will be satisfied to bid and make game in spades.

Most modern bidding aids are intended to discover fit and investigate the strength of the fit. If as dealer you pick up the aforementioned hand:

♠ K 9 8 7 4 2   ♥ A 8   ♦ —   ♣ A Q 9 6 4

you will be delighted if the opponents leave you alone to describe your hand and explore the strength of a possible fit according to your partnership methods. But opponents are aware of the need to compete, and it is all too likely that with long suits and unusual distribution they will make a nuisance of themselves. Instead of your side getting a free run it is quite possible that the bidding will proceed:

1♠	3♦	3♠	5♦

Partner's bid may be based on three or four card support depending on the length shown by the opening bid of 1♠, and his bid may have been made 'under pressure', that is to say he may have stretched to bid at all. The opponents may be bidding 5♦ in the expectation of making it, and if one of them has a void in clubs there may be no defence to 6♦. Equally they may be bidding 5♦ as an advance sacrifice, because they do not think that they can defeat 4♠.

There can be no question of allowing the opponents to play in 5♦ when your hand has such obvious playing strength. A bid of 5♥ is a possibility. There may be some merit in a bid of 6♣, since it will probably be right for partner to lead a club if the opponents bid on. In practice, however, you are likely to take a stab at 5♠ or 6♠, and hope to 'get it right' more often than not.

This is the sort of problem posed in the contested auction. In a team of four match over thirty-two boards, to make the right decision on two or three boards where everyone has joined in the fray is going to be critical.

1♥	1♠	3♥	3♠
4♥	4♠	Pass	Pass
?			

1♦	Dble	1♠	2♥
3♠	4♥	4♠	5♥
Pass	Pass	?	

If you guess wrong on these two boards it may not make much difference whether you are playing Gerber or Roman Blackwood on the remaining thirty. Experts dislike 'guessing', and prefer to call it judgment. Perhaps judgment is the better word, for a player has to judge not only how strong is his own fit and how many tricks his side can take, but also the strength of the opponents' fit and how many tricks they can make.

Judgment or guesswork, call it what you will, the correct way to approach the problem of competitive bidding, in the first instance, is to regard it as a crude rough and tumble where subtlety and inference are reduced to random guesswork. The bidding space that you and your partner have reserved for delicate scientific investigation will be uncouthly gobbled up by rude opponents who pre-empt, deceive, snare you with phantom sacrifices, and make advance sacrifices of their own which turn out not to be sacrifices at all. The more they respect your bidding, the more they will do it; and the only defence is retaliation.

It will be shown in the course of this book that there is a thread through the labyrinth, there is more skill and science in this web of intrigue called competitive bidding than most players realise. But it is essential to recognise from the start that the opponents are there primarily to make a nuisance of themselves. There will be occasions when you are lucky to find your fit at all. Perfect fit is no more than a mirage. For all practical purposes a fit in a contested auction is defined as eight cards or more in a suit, a good fit is nine or more cards.

Chapter 2
The Importance of a Fit

The defensive potential of a hand with a solid six card suit will vary according to partner's holding in the suit; if he has four cards there cannot be more than one defensive trick, whereas if he only has a singleton the suit should produce two or even three defensive tricks. But for the purpose of making a contract yourself it is unlikely to matter how many supporting cards partner has. The suit is self-supporting. Solid suits are easily evaluated in terms of playing tricks, and they are the exception rather than the rule. In the normal course of events the possession of an eight card trump fit is of vital importance. An apparently insignificant hand caused a sizeable swing in a team of four match because of this vital eight card trump fit:

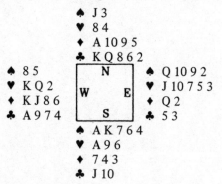

```
                    ♠ J 3
                    ♥ 8 4
                    ♦ A 10 9 5
                    ♣ K Q 8 6 2
    ♠ 8 5          ┌─────────┐     ♠ Q 10 9 2
    ♥ K Q 2        │    N    │     ♥ J 10 7 5 3
    ♦ K J 8 6      │ W     E │     ♦ Q 2
    ♣ A 9 7 4      │    S    │     ♣ 5 3
                   └─────────┘
                    ♠ A K 7 6 4
                    ♥ A 9 6
                    ♦ 7 4 3
                    ♣ J 10
```

The bidding in one room was:

South	West	North	East
1♠	Pass	1NT	Pass
Pass	2♣	Dble	2♦
Dble	Pass	Pass	2♥
Dble	All Pass		

North preferred to bid 1NT instead of 2♣ since his partnership style followed the modern tendency to insist on more rigid requirements for a response at the two level. South was too quick on the trigger, and was caught in the doubling rhythm. The contract was made for a score of 670.

Exchange the two of clubs in the North hand with the two of hearts in the West hand. A casual glance at the diagram reveals no significant alteration. No vital card is changed. East-West still have the critical minor honours in the trump suit. There is no bad trump break. The only difference is that the eight card fit has been removed. Does it matter? Apparently not, but play the hand through, you will see that the probable outcome is 500 to North-South. On this part score hand the extra heart to make an eight card fit is worth 1170 points.

Two equally dramatic examples of the importance of fit occurred in the same rubber recently. Before either side had made a game West dealt as follows:

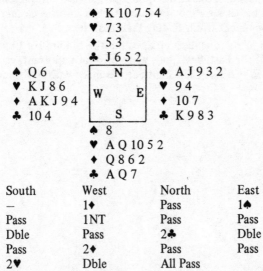

♠ K 10 7 5 4
♥ 7 3
♦ 5 3
♣ J 6 5 2

♠ Q 6
♥ K J 8 6
♦ A K J 9 4
♣ 10 4

♠ A J 9 3 2
♥ 9 4
♦ 10 7
♣ K 9 8 3

♠ 8
♥ A Q 10 5 2
♦ Q 8 6 2
♣ A Q 7

South	West	North	East
—	1♦	Pass	1♠
Pass	1NT	Pass	Pass
Dble	Pass	2♣	Dble
Pass	2♦	Pass	Pass
2♥	Dble	All Pass	

Not only was there no eight card fit for either side, but the cards lay badly for South who conceded 700.

The hand that finished the rubber was:

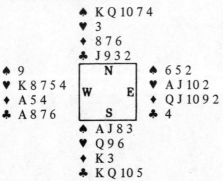

♠ K Q 10 7 4
♥ 3
♦ 8 7 6
♣ J 9 3 2

♠ 9
♥ K 8 7 5 4
♦ A 5 4
♣ A 8 7 6

♠ 6 5 2
♥ A J 10 2
♦ Q J 10 9 2
♣ 4

♠ A J 8 3
♥ Q 9 6
♦ K 3
♣ K Q 10 5

South, an ardent devotee of the point count theory, was still smarting from the earlier debacle, and was eager to get his revenge, particularly against vulnerable opponents. The bidding was:

South	West	North	East
–	Pass	Pass	Pass
1♣	Pass	1♠	Dble
Rdble	2♥	Pass	Pass
Dble	All Pass		

South's redouble of 1♠ was unsound. In this type of situation the redouble, which allows the opponents to bid cheaply, should deny a fit with partner and should express the desire to penalise the opponents. To raise partner's suit has exactly the opposite effect, it informs partner of the fit and inhibits the opponents from finding their best fit.

Regardless of the technical merit of South's bidding, or East's bidding, the cards lay well for East-West; and, what is more important, each side had an eight card fit in two suits. The contract was made with four overtricks.

Chapter 3
The Chances of a Fit

The effects of entering the auction on a deal which turns out to be a total misfit, or proves to be a perfect fit are not always as spectacular as the last two hands. Nonetheless all bridge players are familiar with the disasters and triumphs which result from coming in at the wrong or right moment. Some hands lend themselves to very obvious defensive manoeuvres. A singleton in the opponent's suit and support for the other three suits, a seven-card suit of one's own, five-five in the unbid suits, all present self-evident possibilities of a good fit. However, consider some less obvious situations.

Your hand is:

♠ K J 4   ♥ 9 2   ♦ K 10 8 5 4   ♣ K 8 4

The opponent on your right deals and opens 1♣. On such a poor suit a 1♦ overcall which takes no bidding space from the opponents has nothing to commend it, so you pass. On your left 1♥, pass from partner, 1♠ on your right. The cards seem to be badly placed for them, but of course you pass, and your left hand opponent makes a minimum bid which is passed round to you, either 1NT or 2♣. Would you protect?

If you are tired, demoralised or playing for a penny a hundred, you pass. Assume then that you are involved in a tight team of four match where every IMP counts, or else you are in contention in a big pairs event. If you pass and let the opponents make 1NT or 2♣ when you could have made 2♦, it is a disaster. It will be equally disastrous to blunder in and concede 300, looking foolish in the process. But assuming that you have the courage to risk looking foolish if the occasion demands it, the stakes are 5 IMPs either way, which could swing the match; at pairs a possible top or bottom against a peaceful average.

It is probable that the opponents hold between them some 19-23 points, leaving 7-11 for partner. They have the majority. Their advantage in high card points may be offset by a favourable placing of the honour cards. Seventeen points pulling their full weight will be the equivalent of twenty-one with two finesses wrong. The critical factor will be the quality of partner's diamond support. If the crystal ball could reveal that partner had three or more diamonds, you would bid and expect to win, but if he had less than three diamonds you would probably regret bidding. That is the problem. What are the chances of a fit? Oh for a crystal ball!

Another problem. You open 1♥, and the bidding proceeds: 1♠ - Pass - 2♠, your hand is:

♠ A 7 3   ♥ K Q 10 8 4   ♦ Q 7   ♣ A 9 2

Do you bid again? If you pass it is quite likely that everyone else will do likewise. What can they make, and what can you make? Some players might dismiss the problem, saying that to bid again on a hand such as this smacks of pairs scoring, as though pairs scoring justifies any lunatic overbid. Admittedly the scoring at pairs is such that a bid which wins more often than it loses is a good bid regardless of the cost on the occasions when it does lose. But even at IMP scoring the part-score made in both rooms is the match winner. Also to push opponents to 3♠ and beat them is a small triumph. What would you not give for a crystal ball to foresee the cost of bidding on a hand like this.

Chapter 4
The Crystal Ball ~
Total Distribution

All bridge players are familar with hand patterns, and know various statistical facts about them. The 4-4-3-2 pattern is the commonest, 65 per cent of hands contain a suit of five or more cards, etc., etc. A theorist inventing a system of bidding would undoubtedly refer to the statistics of hand patterns. For they are the raw material of the uncontested auction.

Bridge statisticians rarely bother to include tables of total hand patterns, presumably they are deemed irrelevant. In fact the total pattern of twenty-six cards that you and your partner hold between you is of more relevance to competitive bidding that the single hand pattern.

Out of more than a hundred possible total hand patterns the seventeen listed below are the most common. Those marked with an asterisk are self-repeating, that is, if you and your partner hold an 8-7-6-5 hand, so do the opponents. The remainder occur in pairs. For example, 8-7-7-4 leaves 9-6-6-5 for the opposing side, and vice versa.

8-7-6-5*	23½%
7-7-6-6*	10½%
9-7-6-4*	7%
8-7-7-4)	6½%
9-6-6-5)	6½%
7-7-7-5)	5%
8-6-6-6)	5%
8-8-6-4)	5%
9-7-5-5)	5%
9-8-5-4*	4%
8-8-5-5*	3%
9-8-6-3)	2%
10-7-5-4)	2%
8-8-7-3)	2%
10-6-5-5)	2%
9-7-7-3)	1½%
10-6-6-4)	1½%

The following information can be deduced from this table:

1)   85 per cent of hands contain at least an eight-card fit.
2)   35 per cent of hands contain a good fit of at least nine cards.
3)   If the opponents have no eight-card fit, the odds are 2-1 against your having one.
4)   If the opponents have a fit of exactly eight cards, the odds are 8-1 on a fit for your side of eight cards or more.
5)   You are guaranteed a fit if the opponents have a nine-card fit.
6)   The better their fit, the better is yours.

This concept of total distribution is of vital importance in competitive bidding. Some sequences announce a fit, others deny one. The bidding:

1♣	Pass	2♣	Pass
Pass	?		

is an open invitation to compete. The opponents have found a fit and have subsided at a low level. Double first, and look at your hand afterwards. If you have chosen the wrong moment and the enemy have reserves of playing strength, it will be difficult for them to penalise your indiscretion with their strength massed in one hand, provided you can locate your fit.

Conversely, it can be very dangerous to re-open after the bidding:

1♦	Pass	1♠	Pass
1NT	Pass	Pass	?

If you have a hand which was worth a bid on the first round, it would have been wiser to make it before the opponents knew their own potential. But whether you have a good hand, an average hand, or a weak shapely hand, it would be a mistake to protect. It is a matter of simple arithmetic. The more you have, the less partner has. The weaker the no-trump rebid, the stronger responder may be. This is a non-fit sequence, if the opponents have no fit the odds are 2-1 against a fit for your side, and re-opening the bidding will lose points in the long run.

This brings us back to the first hand in the previous chapter:

♠ K J 4   ♥ 9 2   ♦ K 10 8 5 4   ♣ K 8 4

1♣	Pass	1♥	Pass
1♠	Pass	1NT/2♣	Pass
Pass	?		

Do you protect? The answer is that it depends whether the last bid was 1NT or 2♣. If the bid was 2♣, it is reasonable to suppose that they have a fit. Therefore it is odds of 8-1 on that your side has a fit, and that fit is likely to be in diamonds. If the bid was 1NT, it is of course possible that they have chosen not to play in an eight-card fit, but it would be dangerous to make that assumption. In principle they have no fit, it is odds against partner having as many as three cards in diamonds, and it will cost to come in.

On the second hand:

♠ A 7 3   ♥ K Q 10 8 4   ♦ Q 7   ♣ A 9 2

it looks dangerous to bid again after the bidding: 1♥ - 1♠ - Pass - 2♠ but look at the problem like this. Would you bid again on:

♠ 7   ♥ A Q 10 6 4   ♦ K J 4   ♣ A J 8 3

after the same sequence? You would? Why? Because there is a better chance of a fit? That is not true. Your chances of a fit are the same. The 5-4-3-1 hand looks more promising, but the possibility of a fit can only be judged in the light of the opponent's bidding, and that is the same in each case. What is more, in the first case partner is known to be short in spades, a singleton you hope, but in the second case he may have wasted values in spades. To bid again when partner passes is a risk, but if anything the first hand presents the lesser risk.

There is another consideration. If partner has a maximum pass he may feel constrained to do something violent if you compete again on your own initiative. An Acol player whose opening bid might conceal 19-20 points would perhaps feel nervous on this account. A strong club player who has limited his hand by his failure to open 1♣, would not feel anxious. To that extent the strong club player can often compete the part-score more freely without fear of being misunderstood, but whatever the basic system the point is that a player must consider not only his own distribution, but the likely total distribution.

The need to compete the part-score on the chance of a fit is a common feature of the pairs game. The next deal is typical of the antics of aggressive pairs players.

```
                    ♠ J
                    ♥ K 10 7 6 5 4
                    ♦ 9 3
                    ♣ J 10 7 4
    ♠ K Q 8 7 2   ┌──────────┐   ♠ A 5 3
    ♥ 9           │    N     │   ♥ Q 8 3
    ♦ 8 7 6       │ W     E  │   ♦ A Q 10 2
    ♣ K 9 8 3     │    S     │   ♣ Q 6 2
                  └──────────┘
                    ♠ 10 9 6 4
                    ♥ A J 2
                    ♦ K J 5 4
                    ♣ A 5
```

South	West	North	East
—	—	Pass	1NT
Pass	2♠	Pass	Pass
Dble	Pass	3♥	Pass
Pass	3♠	Pass	Pass
Dble	All Pass		

East-West conceded 300. The first six bids are fairly normal. South's double is dangerous since there is no guarantee that the opponents have an eight-card fit, nevertheless it is highly probable that partner has a small single-ton spade, in which case the hands will fit well. West's bid of 3♠ is not unreasonable, how many match points can he expect from defending against 3♥? South's double of 3♠ is speculative, but who can argue with success?

Bridge players are nurtured on point count theory. It is the obvious elementary way for a beginner to evaluate his hand. The next idea the novice encounters is hand patterns. A 5-5-2-1 hand has greater potential than a 4-3-3-3 shape. But neither point count nor single hand pattern is adequate guidance in a contested auction. Here the concept of total distribution is indispensable.

Consider the following two hands:

a)   ♠ K J 8 6 2   ♥ Q 2   ♦ 4   ♣ K 10 8 5 3

b)   ♠ K J 8 6 2   ♥ Q 2   ♦ A   ♣ K Q 8 5 3

and the bidding:

1♦	Pass	1♥	1♠
1NT	Pass	Pass	?

Both hands have a promising 5-5-2-1 distribution. A beginner would assume that the second hand with the stronger point count is worth a second bid. It is so easy to bid 2♣, and it is so obvious. But it is a mistake. 2♣ will be doubled, dummy will go down with ten red cards, and the contract will be slaughtered. If anything the stronger hand will prove more expensive, for the more you have the less partner has, and there will be no entry to dummy. Your promising 5-5-2-1 hand has been carved up. If you have never heard of total distribution you may moan about your luck and complain how unfair the game is. But whatever made you think it was fair? Your own distribution is no more than a poor guide to the total distribution, and if that is 7-7-6-6, which has an overall frequency of 10 per cent, you aren't going to make many tricks. Nobody is.

It was so easy to bid 2♣ on the last hand, yet it was wrong from the view-point of total distribution. Let us take a similar hand and alter the bidding slightly:

♠ K J 8 6 2   ♥ 5 3   ♦ 4   ♣ A Q 8 5 3

1♦	Pass	1♥	1♠
1NT	Pass	2♦	?

It might have been wiser to double on the first round in preference to bidding 1♠, for now it is extremely difficult to bid 3♣. Non-vulnerable, however, it is not nearly as dangerous as it first appears. The opponents have a diamond fit and the hand is about to be passed out in 2♦. Partner is marked with some values, and he has no liking for spades. If you bid 3♣, get doubled and make it because partner has a nine count with a four-card club suit, the opponents may suspect malpractice. Provided partner has passed smoothly over 1NT there is no malpractice, only the clairvoyance arising from total distribution.

Because it is easy to enter the auction, that does not mean it is right to do so, and conversely, though it is difficult it may still be right to come in. A hand from the 1979 National Pairs Final provided a good illustration of the theory of total distribution:

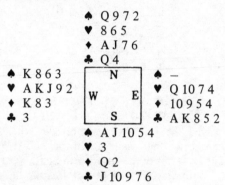

```
                        ♠ Q 9 7 2
                        ♥ 8 6 5
                        ♦ A J 7 6
                        ♣ Q 4
    ♠ K 8 6 3      ┌─────────┐      ♠ —
    ♥ A K J 9 2    │    N    │      ♥ Q 10 7 4
    ♦ K 8 3        │ W     E │      ♦ 10 9 5 4
    ♣ 3            │    S    │      ♣ A K 8 5 2
                   └─────────┘
                        ♠ A J 10 5 4
                        ♥ 3
                        ♦ Q 2
                        ♣ J 10 9 7 6
```

With East-West vulnerable, the bidding was:

South	West	North	East
Pass	1♥	Pass	4♥
4♠	Dble	All Pass	

In view of the opponents' good heart fit, there is almost certainly a black suit fit for North-South, the only question is whether it is clubs or spades. The bid of 4♠ is an acceptable risk, for South has only to make seven tricks at this vulnerability to show a profit. Of course if North has shown any interest in the auction, or has hesitated at any stage, South would be ethically barred from entering the auction on such a hand. As it happened, East, Dave Bretherton, whose manners and ethics are always exemplary, was the only player to face an ethical problem; that was because his partner, Eric Crowhurst, had doubled 4♠ after a considerable amount of thought. After the hand had been played, Bretherton remarked mildly to his partner that it was a pity that he had taken so long to double. Crowhurst, realising the problem, apologised immediately. East would have preferred to try 5♥ rather than accept the probably inadequate penalty from 4♠, but since his partner had doubled after long thought he knew it was right to remove the double, and because his knowledge came partly from his partner's hesitation he felt he was unable to take advantage of it. A newcomer to the game of bridge could be forgiven for thinking such behaviour quixotic, but as tournament players know, this is the standard of ethics which the top players aspire to.

Most players would agree that: 1♣ - Pass 2♣ invites competition, few if any would agree that: 1♠ - Pass - 4♠ also invites competition.

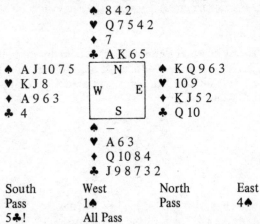

```
                        ♠ 8 4 2
                        ♥ Q 7 5 4 2
                        ♦ 7
                        ♣ A K 6 5
    ♠ A J 10 7 5                           ♠ K Q 9 6 3
    ♥ K J 8            N                    ♥ 10 9
    ♦ A 9 6 3      W       E                ♦ K J 5 2
    ♣ 4                S                    ♣ Q 10
                        ♠ —
                        ♥ A 6 3
                        ♦ Q 10 8 4
                        ♣ J 9 8 7 3 2
```

South	West	North	East
Pass	1♠	Pass	4♠
5♣!	All Pass		

West smoothly played the jack of hearts on the second round of the suit, but declarer guessed right and made eleven tricks. East-West did not like the bidding, and made no secret of it. Since North-South were vulnerable and East-West were not, South was accused of not treating the game seriously, what the hell did he intend to do if 5♣ was doubled. He said he was not frightened of a double by East whose hand was weak defensively, but if West produced a heavy double he would redouble for the red suits!

For the sane reader who believes that South was not being serious, the test is this: collect ten hands where the Acol bidding has been: 1 of a major - 4 of a major, it must be Acol since there has to be a strong presumption that the opponents have a ten-card fit, and analyse the hand afterwards to see if you could have made eight tricks your way. For if eight or more tricks were available, at favourable vulnerability you should have come in. Partner does not assume that the intruder has a three loser hand, if opponents can be induced to play five of a major they must make exactly eleven tricks or risk losing IMPs.

A study of total distribution leads a player to regard the obvious bid with suspicion. Consider this hand as a problem:

♠ A J 8 7 5   ♥ A J 3   ♦ 4 2   ♣ Q 8 4

Left hand opponent deals and opens 1♦ (Precision), partner overcalls 3♣ (Intermediate), and right hand opponent bids 4♠. What do you bid?

There is no doubt that most players would double automatically at the table, and stoutly defend their action afterwards. It would be wrong. Both opponents said they would have run to 5♦ if 4♠ had been doubled, and as can be seen from the layout below declarer can make 6♦ on the right line of play.

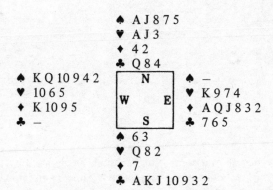

The key to the hand lies in the club holding. You have a nine or ten card club fit, the opponents have a similar fit which you know is not in spades. Therefore their fit is in diamonds. Which would you rather defend, 4♠ undoubled, or 5♦, doubled if you wish?

Chapter 5
TNT

Point count is of no use in a competitive auction. Single hand pattern is an illusion. It is wrong to double the opponents' game contract with three trump tricks and an outside ace when partner has bid. Is there no end to this heretical attack on cherished traditional beliefs? Is there nothing constant upon which to pin one's faith? There is indeed. It is called TNT.

Hands exist where the high card points are more or less evenly divided, neither side has more than seven cards in one suit, and neither side can make a contract above the one level. The deal yields seven tricks for either partnership playing in its best trump suit, fourteen altogether. At the other end of the scale if you and your partner have all the red cards between you, you can make all thirteen tricks, but so can the opponents playing in a black suit. Thirteen tricks, twenty-six altogether. At these two extremes there is a direct relationship between the number of trumps held by each partnership and the number of tricks they can take. What happens in between? The staggering answer is that it still applies. There is a close correlation between the total number of tricks a deal will yield, and the combined trump length of both partnerships. Of course this does not mean that if you have a ten-card spade fit you can take ten tricks; if this were so it would reduce bridge to the intellectual level of pontoon. What it does mean is that if you have a ten-card fit in spades and the opponents have a nine-card heart fit, there is a total of nineteen tricks available on the deal; and if your portion is not the ten, the opponents can make game in hearts. Similarly if they can make twelve tricks in hearts, your portion of the nineteen total tricks is seven, and the sacrifice against their slam will go five down.

You don't believe it? Of course you don't. What self-respecting bridge player would believe such potential dynamite as that without checking it for himself? Check it. Call the total number of tricks the TNT (fairly appropriate), deal three hands, work out the best line of play for either side in its best trump suit, then compare the TNT with the combined trump length (CTL). It won't be more than one out in three deals.

In fact someone has analysed rather more than three deals. A Frenchman, Jean Renes Vernes, went through 2444 deals from the World Championships of 1953 to 1963 and extracted the 340 deals where the hand was played in a different trump suit in the opposite direction when it was replayed in the

other room. He made no attempt to distinguish between good and bad
contracts, mistakes and brilliancies in the play. He compared the actual TNT
with the combined trump length. These were the results he obtained:

In 113 cases the figures matched exactly.

In 88 cases the TNT was less than the combined trump length.

In 139 deals the TNT exceeded the combined trump length.

Out of the 227 deals where the figures did not match, the discrepancy was
only one trick 159 times. In one isolated case the TNT exceeded the CTL by
five. We are left to conjecture whether the defence in both rooms got off to a
disastrous opening lead, or whether the deal was a total freak. Probably both.

The overall figure that emerged was that the TNT exceeded the CTL by
0.275 of a trick taken over 340 deals. Vernes went on to conclude that this
discrepancy of a quarter of a trick was due largely to the declarer's advantage
of seeing both hands.

It is very difficult to believe that this TNT can remain so constant. It
seems so obvious that it must depend on the division of the high cards, the
position of the high cards, and the division of the trumps or side suits. In
principle it is unaffected. Let's look at a hand.

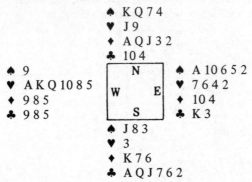

♠ K Q 7 4
♥ J 9
♦ A Q J 3 2
♣ 10 4

♠ 9   ♠ A 10 6 5 2
♥ A K Q 10 8 5   ♥ 7 6 4 2
♦ 9 8 5   ♦ 10 4
♣ 9 8 5   ♣ K 3

♠ J 8 3
♥ 3
♦ K 7 6
♣ A Q J 7 6 2

In both rooms of a team of four match the contract was 5♦ , one down
after a spade ruff. In one room East overcalled 1♠ , and West bid 2♥ . In the
other room East remained silent, and West butted in with 2♥ . In neither
room did East-West see fit to proceed beyond the level of 2♥ .

The hand has all the dramatic appeal of a damp squib, but it does provide
a useful illustration of the TNT theory. East-West have a ten-card heart fit.
North-South have two eight-card fits. More about this later, but two eight-
card fits are usually the equivalent of a nine-card fit. The CTL is 19. As the
cards lie East-West can make nine tricks, North-South can make ten. The TNT
is equal to the CTL.

Let's try and change the hand a little and upset the TNT. Exchange the
king of clubs with a small club from the West hand. A contract of 4♥ by
West is unbeatable, but North goes another trick off in 5♦ , and the TNT is

unaltered. What kills 5♦ is the spade ruff. Remove it. Give West the two of spades in exchange for a small card in one of the minors. North can now make his contract of five diamonds, but the TNT remains the same because West can only make eight tricks in hearts. Let's create another singleton for East-West, surely that will upset the apple cart. Trade the four of diamonds with the five of clubs, that must increase the TNT, the 4-1 trump break won't hurt North who can take a force in the short trump hand, and it will remove a loser for West. Not so. Best defence may be difficult to find, but an opening trump lead leaves West with three diamond losers and only two trumps to ruff them with. That wretched TNT still refuses to change. What about a void? Move the three of hearts to North in exchange for the four of spades. Still no good, North makes a trick more, but West has developed a trump loser via a trump promotion.

On the previous hand the TNT worked very neatly, both sides could make a part-score of their own, there were no voids, no bad trump breaks, neither side had a preponderance of high cards or distributional values. Would the TNT really work so well if one side could make a slam?

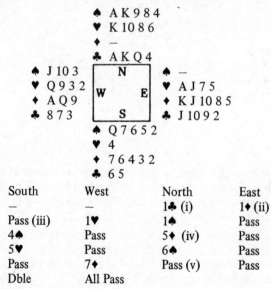

	South	West	North	East
	—	—	1♣ (i)	1♦ (ii)
	Pass (iii)	1♥	1♠	Pass
	4♠	Pass	5♦ (iv)	Pass
	5♥	Pass	6♠	Pass
	Pass	7♦	Pass (v)	Pass
	Dble	All Pass		

(i)   Strong club
(ii) Red two-suiter
(iii) 0-3 points
(iv) Asking for a cue-bid in the next suit up
(v)   Inviting the grand with a void heart

Since the sacrifice cost 1300, everyone looked eagerly at the hand after-wards to see if the vulnerable slam would have made. On careful play it would have. If East does not cash his ace of hearts, he does not make it; if he does, North has only three losers to ruff. The TNT, then, was twelve plus six. It should have been nineteen, counting two eight-card fits as a nine-card fit. The explanation of that was that East lost a trick in the play. If he plays one trump, and a heart finesse, and then plays patiently on clubs, he must come to seven tricks.

Chapter 6
The Accuracy of TNT

A non-bridge playing statistician asked to investigate the relationship between point count and tricks taken over a statistically significant number of deals would conclude:

The positive correlation is sufficently strong to suggest that there is a direct relationship between point count and tricks taken. However the statistical variation from the expected norm is such that, over a limited number of deals, point count would be unreliable as a guide to tricks taken.

The same statistician analysing the correlation between total number of tricks, combined trump length, and the division of points between opposing partnerships would report:

The correlation between TNT and CTL is exact within normal statistical variations; between TNT and the division of points, no correlation.

Expressed in common language this means that in the contested auction, applying the rule of TNT is similar to trying to tell the time by an ungraduated hour glass, using point count is equivalent to looking at the sun.

There is hardly a rule or precept at bridge which is not broken at some time. The art of the game lies in knowing when to break the rules, and foreseeing when the rules will not apply. If TNT is sometimes inaccurate, is this inaccuracy predictable?

Most players will recall hands where declarer is doubled and encounters a bad trump break missing some trump honour and an apparently insiginificant card such as the nine or ten of trumps. With the nine or ten of trumps the hand is under control, but without it, in an effort to make an unmakeable contract, declarer loses control, and crashes in a spectacular fashion. That nine of trumps is totally useless to the opposition playing in their own best trump suit, yet in defence it may be worth a huge penalty. Though it may be instinctively distasteful, perhaps declarer should concentrate on restricting the penalty on hands like this, but there is no legislating for the importance of the nine of trumps in the bidding. It is unpredictable.

Vernes gives three predictable factors which affect the accuracy of the rule of TNT.

1   The Existence of a Double Fit

When both sides have a fit of eight or more cards in each of two suits, the TNT is one more than expected. Thus, of the self-repeating hand patterns 9-8-5-4 is likely to produce one trick more than 9-7-6-4. As has been suggested already 10-6-5-5 leaves the opponents two eight-card fits, and gives a TNT of nineteen, exactly the same as the 10-6-6-4 pattern which gives a nine-card fit in the opposite direction.

Vernes found that the double fit was the most frequent cause of an increase in TNT.

2   The Possession of Trump Honours

When each side holds all the honours in its trump suit the TNT is frequently one higher than expected. When the defenders have trump honours the TNT will sometimes be lower. Note that in the first hand in the previous chapter neither side had trump losers. It was only when the trumps were stacked with three to the jack offside and promotable that the TNT was altered. Bear in mind also that if you have all of the trump honours you are unlikely to worried about the position of the nine or ten of trumps, but if you are missing one or more trump honours you may be very concerned about a bad trump break or the position of the ten or nine.

3   The Division of the Side Suits

One would expect this to have a dramatic effect on the TNT. Vernes found this to be the least important of the three factors. Clearly if your own short suits are divided 4-1, 4-2, or 5-1 between the two hands rather than 3-2 or 3-3 you will have less losers, but equally you will have better defensive prospects. The TNT is largely unaltered.

The two hands that follow are worth study since they both show a dramatic divergence from the rule of TNT.

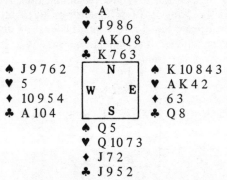

```
                    ♠ A
                    ♥ J 9 8 6
                    ♦ A K Q 8
                    ♣ K 7 6 3
    ♠ J 9 7 6 2        N        ♠ K 10 8 4 3
    ♥ 5                         ♥ A K 4 2
    ♦ 10 9 5 4      W     E     ♦ 6 3
    ♣ A 10 4          S         ♣ Q 8
                    ♠ Q 5
                    ♥ Q 10 7 3
                    ♦ J 7 2
                    ♣ J 9 5 2
```

At one table in a team of four match North opened 1♥, East overcalled 1♠, South 2♥, West 2♠. North bid 4♥, and East bid 4♠ which was passed to North who passed reluctantly after some consideration.

The lead was a heart won by the ace, and a small heart ruff allowed dummy to play trumps. North won the ace and cashed the ace of diamonds. Declarer played the six in an effort to disrupt the defenders' signals, but fortunately for South he was able to contribute the two. North switched back to hearts. Declarer eliminated the hearts and ran the trumps down to a three-card end position. Risking the overtrick, North avoided the endplay by throwing his king and queen of diamonds. Though the defence was spectacular, the result was fairly normal.

At the other table North opened a multi-coloured 2♦. East overcalled 2♠, South passed, and West bid 4♠. North, who felt that he had not yet had his say, doubled. South decided to take the double out. It is one of the built-in disadvantages of the Roman 2♦ bid that the relative strengths of partner's suits is unknown. If South had put a tentative toe on 5♣, there might have been no story, but as it was South opted for 5♥. When this came round to East he had no problem, he doubled.

The lead was a spade, won by the ace. The eight of trumps won the next trick, and declarer realised that he might lose his spade ruff if he played another trump. He played a club from dummy which went to the jack and ace. A diamond was returned. Declarer won with the jack, ruffed his spade, and led a trump. At this point the roof fell in and declarer emerged from the debris with six tricks and a loss of 900 points.

The total number of tricks on the deal was fifteen. Four short of expectation. What has gone wrong? First, the declarer in 5♥ has lost two tricks in the play. After winning the eight of trumps he can play on the minors and settle for three off, losing two club and three trumps. That accounts for two of the tricks. Let us try to explain away the other two.

With J-9-8-6 opposite Q-10-7-3 only two trump losers are expected, but declarer has to lose to the four of trumps in order to avoid losing control.

To explain the disappearance of the remaining trick requires a deeper analysis. By judiciously changing a few honour cards, a slightly different deal can be obtained. Each hand has the same point count and distribution. Each side possesses the same number of aces, kings, queens and jacks.

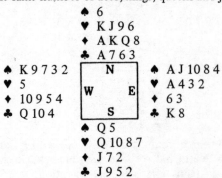

East-West make ten tricks in spades. A brief glance suggests that North-South lose only four tricks in a heart contract, making the TNT nineteen as expected. In fact by witholding his ace of trumps East can force declarer to develop an apparently unnecessary trump loser in exactly the same way as on the actual hand. Of course, if one is intent upon proving the infallibility of TNT, it is possible to indulge in a little dishonest sleight of hand and transfer the ten of clubs to the North hand. Then the TNT is indeed nineteen.

The explanation of the loss of a trick lies partly in the possession of each other's trump honours. On the first hand the ace and queen of trumps did no harm to East's spade contract, but they were wasted values in South's heart contract. The king of hearts was of no value to East except in defence. On the re-arranged layout, North-South have two effective trump suits, hearts and clubs. The ten of clubs is a vital trump honour, since there are other trump honours missing.

On the second hand the TNT swings wildly in the other direction.

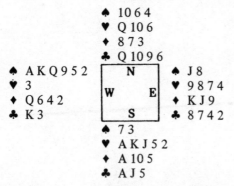

♠ 10 6 4
♥ Q 10 6
♦ 8 7 3
♣ Q 10 9 6

♠ A K Q 9 5 2   ♠ J 8
♥ 3   ♥ 9 8 7 4
♦ Q 6 4 2   ♦ K J 9
♣ K 3   ♣ 8 7 4 2

♠ 7 3
♥ A K J 5 2
♦ A 10 5
♣ A J 5

South opened 1♥ after two passes and West butted in with 4♠ which was doubled by South. West was well pleased with the little gems that his partner gave him, and made ten tricks with the aid of a club finesse and a diamond break.

When the hand was replayed, South opened a strong club, West bid 3♠ which came back to South who doubled. North bid 4♣, and there they stayed. West started with three rounds of spades. Declarer ruffed and led the jack of clubs, making ten tricks.

Twenty tricks in all, yet the spades are eight cards, and the club length is seven. Five tricks out.

It is curious quirk of the game of bridge that by playing in a 4-3 fit and taking the force in the short hand it is possible to make more tricks than one would expect. Note that in a more normal heart contract there are only nine tricks to be taken even on imperfect defence. On best defence South can only make eight tricks, the combined heart length is eight, and the TNT is only two adrift. But those two cannot be explained away. Such things happen. They are likely to happen when each side possesses its own trump honours and has a perfect fit in two suits, fit being used in its secondary sense of honours in partner's side suit. From West's point of view, if he had found his partner with king, jack of hearts instead of king, jack of diamonds he would have been less pleased and the TNT would have been normal.

Chapter 7
TNT and
the Losing Trick Count

There is a close relationship between the rule of TNT and the Losing Trick Count. TNT is a sort of corollary of the losing count applied to all four hands. Consequently it is helpful to study the losing count in order to understand TNT.

There are twelve top cards, but thirteen tricks to be taken. So according to the losing count, there is always an unclaimed trick.

♠ K Q 8	N	♠ A 7 3 2
♥ K 7 5 2	W E	♥ A Q 6
♦ A Q 4		♦ K J 5
♣ K Q 3	S	♣ A 9 4

West has five losers, East has seven losers. By adding seven and five, and subtracting from the magic figure of eighteen, the answer of six emerges. East-West can make a contract at the six level. On a completely flat hand such as this, twelve of the available thirteen tricks will be taken by the twelve top honours. The thirteenth is in dispute. It will be won by a major suit jack or a long card in either major. The addition of either critical major suit jack to the East or West hand would settle the issue immediately. But 7NT is a good contract since it will make on one of two even breaks or a squeeze. On this hand, as on most other no-trump type hands, the unclaimed trick goes to the partnership with the preponderance of high cards. That is the partnership which has the greater opportunity to establish the small cards in its long suits.

In a trump suit distributional values can fulfil the same function as high cards. West has:

♠ K Q 10 8 3   ♥ A 9 4   ♦ 7 2   ♣ A 8 2

a sound opening bid containing the expected seven losers. Whether East has:

♠ A 9 5 2   ♥ K Q 3   ♦ A 8 4   ♣ J 7 5

or

♠ A 9 7 5 4 2   ♥ 3   ♦ A 8 4   ♣ J 7 5

the deal will produce ten tricks in spades. There is no wastage of values, and the singleton heart is equivalent to the king and queen. Both the responding hands are nominally eight loser hands, which would suggest a contract at the three level, but in fact the unclaimed trick goes to the side which has a good trump fit. This phenomenon is often referred to as deducting a loser for trump control.

A simple example of trump control is a trump suit divided A-9-6-3-2 opposite K-8-7-5-4. Each hand counts two losers in the suit, a total of four, leaving one overall loser in that suit, yet this loser is absorbed in the combined power of the trump suit, and is no longer expected.

Trump control is not always as simple as the mere possession of ten trumps. A more comprehensive definition would be 'the possession of sufficient trumps to be able to take full advantage of the distributional features of the combined hands'. The word sufficient requires some elaboration.

♠ A 8 5	N	♠ K 9 4 2
♥ A Q J 7 6 3	W E	♥ K 9 5
♦ A		♦ K 8 5 4 2
♣ J 9 7	S	♣ 8

Only an exact card slam can succeed with such a low point count. According to the losing count there are six losers opposite seven, which indicates a contract at the five level. A trump lead robs declarer of trump control, he no longer has sufficient trumps to ruff his losing clubs. But without a trump lead declarer has trump control, which is worth the extra trick. If responder has one less diamond and one more trump, now there are sufficient trumps to ensure the slam. Counting the singleton as one loser presupposes that partner has losers in that suit which need to be ruffed, and that there are sufficient trumps to do the job.

What constitutes sufficient and good enough trumps to deduct a loser will vary from hand to hand. Consider:

♠ K 9 3 2   ♥ A K 8   ♦ A 4   ♣ Q 7 6 5

which opens a strong no-trump, and suppose partner shows a five-card heart suit with slam interest. Since the strong no-trump announces the equivalent of six losers, presumably partner has six losers or a promising seven loser hand. If he has:

♠ A 8 7   ♥ Q J 9 5 4   ♦ K 8 2   ♣ A J

there is an excellent slam in spite of his seven losers. Trump control consists of having a small trump to ruff his diamond loser, and his jack of clubs proves to be a vital card.

If he has the potentially stronger hand:

♠ A 8 7   ♥ Q J 9 5 4   ♦ K Q 2   ♣ A 4

which contains only six losers, the slam, though still playable on a finesse or a squeeze, is not as good as on the previous seven loser hand, there is no trump control, since the doubleton diamond is a wasted feature. To regain the trump control opener must have one less spade and one more trump.

♠ K 9 3	N	♠ A 8 7
♥ A K 8 7	W E	♥ Q J 9 5 4
♦ A 4		♦ K Q 2
♣ Q 7 6 5	S	♣ A 4

Now there are adequate trumps since the doubleton diamond can be converted into a doubleton spade, and the slam is virtually unbeatable.

This will o' the wisp called trump control can play some strange tricks.

♠ A Q J 8 5 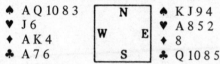 ♠ K 9 4
♥ K 9 5 2   ♥ A Q J 8
♦ J 8 2   ♦ A 5 3
♣ 6   ♣ A 7 2

East has the 4-3-3-3 shape which is valued so pessimistically by the losing count. It is correct to deduct a loser if the controls are good. This hand is certainly equivalent to the average six loser hand. West has seven losers. Seven losers facing six amounts to eleven tricks with no trump control, and that is the number of tricks with spades as trumps, but played in hearts a grand slam is a good contract. Trump control is worth two tricks.

It is extremely rare that trump control should add two tricks. Much more frequently the losing count will overestimate, and the hand will produce a trick less than expected. There are three reasons why this will happen: duplication of values, duplication of losers, and duplication of hand pattern.

1 Duplication of Values

♠ A Q 10 8 3 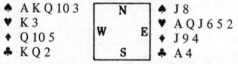 ♠ K J 9 4
♥ J 6   ♥ A 8 5 2
♦ A K 4   ♦ 8
♣ A 7 6   ♣ Q 10 8 5

In spite of the thirteen losers, 5♠ depends on the club position because of the duplication of values in diamonds. With the minor suits reversed there may be an overtrick in 6♠.

2 Duplication of Losers

♠ A K Q 10 3 ┌─N─┐ ♠ J 8
♥ K 3   W   E ♥ A Q J 6 5 2
♦ Q 10 5   └─S─┘ ♦ J 9 4
♣ K Q 2   ♣ A 4

Eleven losers, the material for a grand slam unless the opponents are unkind enough to cash two diamond tricks.

3 Duplication of Hand Pattern

♠ Q 9 3   ┌─N─┐ ♠ A J 2
♥ A Q J 4 2   W   E ♥ K 9 8 7 6
♦ A 8   └─S─┘ ♦ K 5
♣ Q 7 2   ♣ K 6 5

In spite of the losing count 5♥ will probably fail. Even 4♥ could fail without the jack of spades. Reversing the minor suits destroys the duplication and 5♥ is safe.

TNT relates directly to the losing count. It loses its accuracy for exactly the same three reasons as the losing count.

1   Duplication of Values

At game all partner deals and opens 1♠, which is doubled on the right. Your hand is:

♠ Q 7 6 5 2   ♥ A 3   ♦ K   ♣ Q 8 7 3 2

The singleton king of diamonds may not be a good feature, but nevertheless you raise to 4♠ with a certain amount of confidence. The opponents find the inspired defence of ace of clubs and a club ruff, and partner emerges with nine tricks only. Rather unlucky, his hand was:

♠ K J 10 4 3   ♥ 9 4 2   ♦ A   ♣ K J 10 4

The losing count errs by two tricks. That each hand should contain a singleton diamond is in itself a duplication of values. When the singletons are the ace and king, the duplication is monstrous. But before feeling too sorry for yourself you should reflect that if 4♠ fails there can be no defence to 5♦, regardless of the layout of the opponents' cards.

In fact the full hand was:

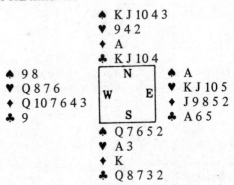

West was very chicken hearted not to enter the bidding.

The deal yields nine tricks in spades, eleven in diamonds, a total of twenty. But the combined trump length is twenty-one with double fits. TNT is two short of expectation just as the losing count is. This ties in with Vernes' analysis of honours in each other's suits.

2 Duplication of Losers

Duplication of values and losers go hand in hand.

North-South Game

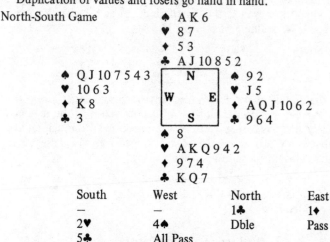

```
                    ♠ A K 6
                    ♥ 8 7
                    ♦ 5 3
                    ♣ A J 10 8 5 2
♠ Q J 10 7 5 4 3    ┌─────────┐   ♠ 9 2
♥ 10 6 3            │    N    │   ♥ J 5
♦ K 8              │ W     E │   ♦ A Q J 10 6 2
♣ 3                │    S    │   ♣ 9 6 4
                    └─────────┘
                    ♠ 8
                    ♥ A K Q 9 4 2
                    ♦ 9 7 4
                    ♣ K Q 7
```

South	West	North	East
–	–	1♣	1♦
2♥	4♠	Dble	Pass
5♣	All Pass		

South did well to bid 5♣ rather than 5♥, since 5♥ would fail on a trump promotion, and 4♠ doubled would yield only 500.

It is customary to count one loser only in a long suit headed by A-J-10 if the rest of the controls are good. North has a poor six loser hand. South has five losers. Clearly North-South cannot make thirteen tricks because of the duplication of losers in diamonds. This duplication of losers is not apparent in the bidding, but if there is a duplication of values it is highly probable that there will be an attendant duplication of losers. North's double of 4♠ acts as a warning of duplication of values, and South is warned off the slam. In fact the losing count was justified to some extent when East led a spade and North made all thirteen tricks.

The TNT is eighteen instead of the expected twenty. It has failed by two tricks for precisely the same reason as the losing trick count failed.

The next hand is a partner of the previous one.

Love All

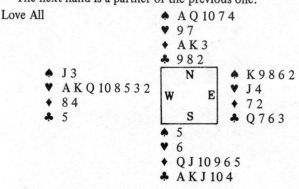

```
                    ♠ A Q 10 7 4
                    ♥ 9 7
                    ♦ A K 3
                    ♣ 9 8 2
♠ J 3              ┌─────────┐   ♠ K 9 8 6 2
♥ A K Q 10 8 5 3 2 │    N    │   ♥ J 4
♦ 8 4              │ W     E │   ♦ 7 2
♣ 5                │    S    │   ♣ Q 7 6 3
                    └─────────┘
                    ♠ 5
                    ♥ 6
                    ♦ Q J 10 9 6 5
                    ♣ A K J 10 4
```

North-South were playing canape, which can produce interesting problems in a contested auction. As a general principle it is usually correct to complete a reverse in competition even if this entails bidding at a higher level than originally intended. The bidding was:

South	West	North	East
—	—	1♠	Pass
2♣	4♥	Dble	All Pass

In view of the double of 4♥, South decided not to complete his reverse at the five level. Partner could have all sorts of useless values in the majors, it was all too likely that the losing count would break down through duplication. The double of 4♥ was wrong. There was no justification for prejudicing a decision which rightly belonged to partner.

In fact the losing count worked perfectly well since the wastage of values was negligible, and consequently TNT also worked perfectly, providing the expected answer of twenty.

3 Duplication of Hand Pattern

This is the most disastrous type of duplication. Fortunately it is rare. Amongst the common total hand patterns it can only occur in three cases: 8-6-6-6, 8-8-6-4 and 10-6-6-4. These three total hand patterns have a combined frequency of 11½ per cent, and even when they do occur the duplicated single hand is vastly against the odds. For all practical purposes duplicated hand patterns cannot be detected in the bidding. There is one exception worth mentioning. Some players sacrifice the natural bid of 3NT over one of a major to show a raise to four of that major with precisely a 4-3-3-3 distribution. On the rare occasions when there is exact duplication of hand pattern opener can pass 3NT and sometimes score a resounding success.

The hand that follow illustrates the catastrophic effects of duplication of hand pattern.

East-West Game

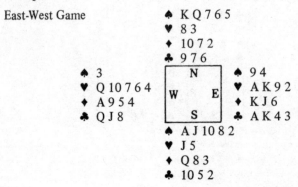

South	West	North	East
—	—	—	1♥
1♠	3♥	3♠	4♥
Pass	Pass	4♠	Dble
All Pass			

East won two heart tricks, tried the underlead of the ace, king of clubs, cashed the clubs and exited with a trump, leaving South to play the diamonds himself. The hand is a museum piece; the total number of tricks is three short of expectation.

If he intends to bid 4♠ on his hand, North should have done so on the first round. It will still cost 900 if it is doubled, but it is less likely to be doubled. In the chapter on TNT raises, North's actions will be heartily condemned.

Chapter 8
The Application of TNT

By dwelling on the inaccuracies of the losing trick count and the consequent discrepancies in the rule of TNT, it is possible to lose sight of the basic accuracy and simplicity of the rule that has emerged.

Partner's bid will nearly always indicate his minimum trump length, so that it is possible to estimate your combined trump length with a fair degree of accuracy. It is not always so easy to guess the opponents' trump length, but the concept of total distribution acts as a statistical forecast of their trump length based on the knowledge of your own, and in the absence of more reliable information, a good practical guide is to assume that their trump length is the same as yours. Therefore as a set of simple everyday rules:

1 If you bid an eight-card fit to the two level it will be difficult for the opponents to extract an adequate penalty even though they have the balance of points, because someone can make eight tricks, and if you can only make seven, they could have made nine.

2 If you have a nine-card fit it is in your interests to bid to the three level, someone can make nine tricks, and that someone might be you.

3 With a ten-card fit, provided you are not heavily outgunned in high card strength, you should bid up to the four level. If your contract does not make the opposition has missed something.

As a recipe for success at the bridge table this formula is so ridiculously simple that most players would instinctively reject it. Let us set up an experiment to test its validity. At equal vulnerability partner opens a weak two in spades and you have:

$$\spadesuit K862 \quad \heartsuit 9 \quad \diamondsuit Q75 \quad \clubsuit A9864$$

There is a ten-card fit your way, which guarantees at least two eight-card fits or a nine-card fit for the opponents. The TNT is nineteen, possibly more if the opponents have a better than average fit. You must raise to 4♠, for if it does not make the opponents have a four level contract, which looks as if it could be hearts. If you are schooled in point count theory you may feel nervous about bidding game on such thin values. Here is the experiment:

Draw this hand from a deck of cards. Ask partner to sort out a typical weak two in spades from the remaining stock. Deal out the remainder to the opponents. Check who can make what.

No test could be fairer, but if you do not like the conclusion of one hand, repeat the experiment.

The power of the eight-card fit at the two level is shown by the next hand.

Love All, IMPs, you hold:

♠ A J 6   ♥ K 5 2   ♦ A 9 4   ♣ K 10 8 4

You open 1♣ and the bidding proceeds:

South	West	North	East
–	1♣	Pass	1♥
1♠	1NT	2♦	2♥
Pass	Pass	2♠	Pass
Pass	?		

What would you do? Although partner does not necessarily have anything in reserve you can assume that you have the majority of the points. Consider your action before studying the full deal:

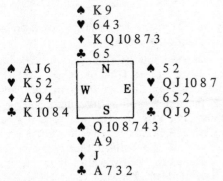

```
                    ♠ K 9
                    ♥ 6 4 3
                    ♦ K Q 10 8 7 3
                    ♣ 6 5
      ♠ A J 6          N          ♠ 5 2
      ♥ K 5 2                     ♥ Q J 10 8 7
      ♦ A 9 4     W        E      ♦ 6 5 2
      ♣ K 10 8 4        S         ♣ Q J 9
                    ♠ Q 10 8 7 4 3
                    ♥ A 9
                    ♦ J
                    ♣ A 7 3 2
```

What are the mathematics of a double which in practice scores −570?

West knows that he has an eight-card fit, and if both sides have an eight-card fit the TNT is probably sixteen. When 2♠ goes two down for +300, ten tricks should be available in hearts for +420. If it goes one down for +100, 3♥ should make for +140. If 2♠ is a make for −470, 3♥ is one off for −50. And these figures assume that partner has only five hearts. If he has six which is likely, the double becomes an even worse proposition because the TNT is higher. On this hand you may curse the opponents for being so annoying, but you must bid on. In fact many of the conventions suggested later are based on this idea, that if you can get into the bidding and find an eight-card fit at the two level, you will force the opponents to bid against the odds whatever they do.

In a contested auction there is nearly always at least one player who can gain a great deal of insight by applying the rule of TNT. Consider the following hand from a team of four match.

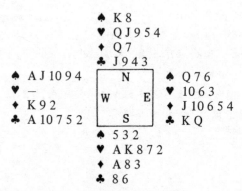

In one room the auction was not contested:

West	East
1♣	1♦
1♠	1NT
2♠	

It is not an easy game to reach, but it might have been bid if East had bid 2♠ instead of 1NT, or raised 2♠ to 3♠.

In the other room North-South held the view that any excuse to overcall at the one level was a good excuse. Over 1♣, North put in 1♥. East, who was not playing Sputnik, could not find anything to say. Now South was the player who had seen the secret scrolls. With a presumed ten-card fit the TNT was nineteen or more. For with top cards in partner's bid suit there was unlikely to be any devaluation. Someone could make a contract at the four level. 4♥ went round to East who doubled. Clearly she did not believe in four level contracts on a combined twenty count. It is interesting to speculate whether she would have doubled 3♥.

There is no doubt that 4♥ is the correct TNT bid on the South hand, designed to achieve par. But can 4♥ be made? Which is more likely, that 4♥ is a make, or that East-West can make four of a black suit? If partner's overcall at the one level is fragile, 4♥ will not make, in which case four of a black suit will. What are the chances that West will come to life again after a raise to 3♥ or a game try? This is the crux of the problem. It is easy to over-rate the opposition, forgetting that they may have difficult decisions. It does require courage to re-open at the three level opposite a passing partner. A bid of 3♥ will probably buy the contract.

This is a recurring theme arising from TNT theory. You know that the opponents have something on, but you must consider carefully what their chances are of finding it.

Partner opens a multi 2♦, showing, amongst other more unlikely types of hand, a weak two in a major. You have a hand very similar to the hand at the beginning of the chapter:

♠ K 8 6 2   ♥ Q 7 5   ♦ 10 3   ♣ A 9 7 6

The next hand passes. So far, so good. You are prepared to go to three of partner's major, so you bid 2NT. This gets past LHO, and partner makes a rebid showing a weak two in spades. Still no sign of life from RHO. Should you hoist to 4♠, or settle for 3♠? What are the chances of making 4♠, and what are the chances of the opponents coming in at this late stage and settling in their best spot? Leave it at 3♠ and take the money.

This general principle of bidding a nine- or ten-card fit to the appropriate level must be tempered with common sense. Several unpleasant things can result from bidding without a certain quota of high card strength. The most obvious is that partner will misjudge the situation and bid again. Equally disastrously, the enemy may be goaded into bidding a makeable game which they would not otherwise have reached. Though they may only have bid it according to the old adage 'when in doubt bid one more of your own suit', what happens is that partner doubles, one of his high cards gets ruffed, and the contract makes, perhaps with an overtrick. The third unfortunate outcome is that you bid to, say 3♠, which fails by one trick due to the cards lying badly, you think this is a fair result because the opponents can make three of a red suit, but on opening the traveller you find you have exchanged +110 for −50. They were not coming in over 2♠.

An unusual variation on this theme occurred recently in a team of four match. Right hand opponent deals and opens 1♦, and you hold:

♠ Q 7   ♥ A K Q J 3   ♦ A 9 8 2   ♣ 8 3

1NT seems no worse than the alternatives, and the bidding continues, rather surprisingly, double, 2♥, pass. According to TNT someone can make something at the four level, and it is in your interests to raise to 4♥, but is this really sensible? This is certain to convert a plus into a minus score when there is no guarantee that the opponents are going to find their best contract. As it happened 2♥ was passed out, the full hand being:

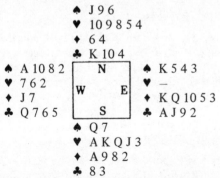

```
              ♠ J 9 6
              ♥ 10 9 8 5 4
              ♦ 6 4
              ♣ K 10 4
♠ A 10 8 2    ┌─────────┐    ♠ K 5 4 3
♥ 7 6 2       │    N    │    ♥ —
♦ J 7         │ W     E │    ♦ K Q 10 5 3
♣ Q 7 6 5     │    S    │    ♣ A J 9 2
              └─────────┘
              ♠ Q 7
              ♥ A K Q J 3
              ♦ A 9 8 2
              ♣ 8 3
```

If declarer in a spade contract does everything right he can make eleven tricks, and the TNT is as expected. In practice the result in the other room was 2♠ + 2. Their bidding also afforded a good illustration of TNT in action. What competitive hand does not? The bidding started: 1♦ - 1♥ - 1♠. North, for all his paucity of high cards was the player who knew more about total tricks than anyone else. Here a little knowledge is a dangerous thing. If he hoists to some number of hearts, not even 4♥ will be sufficient to silence East who will bid the appropriate number of spades for fear of being talked out of something. Then when the hearts have been bid and raised, West will not need to be unusually endowed with perspicacity to realise that his partner is short of hearts, and his own hand has been improved by the bidding. North astutely passed, East bid a conservative 2♠, and there they stayed. One of the benefits of a proper understanding of TNT is that you try to avoid helping the opponents to bid their hands.

Before leaving this hand, observe the effect of exchanging the king and queen of hearts with the ten and nine. North's hand is now:

♠ J 9 6   ♥ K Q 8 5 4   ♦ 6 4   ♣ K 10 4

and the bidding has been: 1♦ - 1♥ - 1♠ - ?

What an interesting sidelight on conventional bidding theory! If you bid on this hand you are going to drive the opponents into a makeable game which they would not otherwise have bid. Of course everyone bids 3♥ on this hand, it would be eccentric not to. What more clearcut decision could you have according to accepted bidding theory? But that is a reflection upon the inadequacy of accepted bidding theory which relates only to your own best contract without regard to total tricks. If the spades are 4-4 or 5-4, 3♥ is a losing bid. Bid 4♥ or pass, but don't bid 3♥. 1NT is a better bid than 3♥!

The player who sees the magic light of TNT piercing the gloom must be sure to take advantage of it. Often the risk of misleading partner is outweighed by the need to fool the opposition. You hold:

♠ 8 7   ♥ K 5 2   ♦ K 9 6 2   ♣ J 10 4 3

and the bidding is: 1♥ - 2♦ - Pass - ?

If it is your lucky day the opening bid is 11-19, and the pass is 0-8. The TNT is high and you have no defence to an opposing game, but do they know that? You must not pass, 3♦ is no use either. 2NT is the bid. Partner will expect a partial diamond fit, and some 10-13 points. He will freely raise to 3NT with a good suit and a sound overcall, or he may retreat to 3♦ in the knowledge that he can expect some measure of tolerance for diamonds, or else extra values. A no-trump contract may not make, but if partner has six diamonds to the ace, jack, that already gives seven tricks on a heart lead.

The gambit here was to conceal the fit. If you wish to indulge in a little deceit rather than just being nice and bidding your points, it can also be winning tactics to claim a fit which does not exist. This is an old rubber bridge ploy that hardly ever fails to bring in 800 on the last rubber.

You hold:

♠ A J 9 6   ♥ K Q 7   ♦ 9 8 5 2   ♣ J 4

and the bidding goes: 1♥ - 1♠ - ?

A bid of 3♥ might not appeal to the purists who would like to have a fourth heart for the bid. But it is almost inevitable that the bidding will proceed: 3♠ - 4♥ - 4♠. In fact if you have one less heart and one more club there is no difference except that the opponents pay a bit more for the privilege of playing in 4♠ doubled.

A similar sort of situation occurs after the bidding: 1♣ - 1♠ - Pass - ? If the opponents expect a raise to 2♠ on a hand such as:

♠ Q 9 4 3   ♥ J 2   ♦ Q 8 7 4 2   ♣ 5 3

or

♠ Q 9 4   ♥ K J 6 5 2   ♦ J 8 7   ♣ 9 2

they may well stretch to re-open. If that is the case, try them out with a raise to 2♠ on:

♠ K 4   ♥ Q 9 4   ♦ K J 8 7   ♣ J 10 3 2

and apply the hammer if they do re-open. You will be surprised how few tricks they make.

Chapter 9
TNT Raises

You hold:

♠ K 10 7 6 5   ♥ 9   ♦ Q 4 3   ♣ J 8 5 4

and partner opens 1♠. Your methods are that an opening one bid shows 11-19 points, and there is a 95 per cent presumption that 1♠ is based on a five-card suit. What do you bid?

If you knew that the opponents would remain silent you would raise to 2♠. That is all the hand is worth constructively. If your methods allow you to raise to 3♠ on these slender distributional values, presumably partner will proceed with due caution.

The situation changes somewhat if the right hand opponent enters the bidding with a take-out double. A raise to 3♠ cannot be misunderstood since the bid of 2NT was available to show a full strength raise to three of partner's suit.

The value of the hand changes once again if the opponents bid to 4♥. Unless partner is well schooled on the type of hand with which to double, the correct action is to bid 4♠. In all probability someone can make a contract at the four level.

This quite ordinary hand is worth 2♠ constructively, 3♠ pre-emptively, and 4♠ competitively.

It is an accepted axiom of the game that a player should raise immediately to the full value of the fit. But TNT theory questions the meaning of 'the full value of the fit'. When partner makes a double or triple raise in a competitive situation, he may be doing so for one of two reasons. Either because he thinks the contract can be made more often or not, or because he is not sure which side has the balance of distributional values, but knows that it is in his interest to bid to that level. For the purposes of reference let us define the second type of raise as a TNT raise.

Disaster will almost certainly ensue if partner interprets a TNT raise as a game invitation or a full value raise. Instead of bidding the full value of your own hand, either to a thin lucky game or a cheap save, and perhaps pushing the opponents overboard, what will happen is that partner will dive overboard himself. If at favourable vulnerability you bid 4♠ as a small insurance policy on the hand above, it is almost inevitable that partner will produce 4NT and register a totally unnecessary minus score.

Another aspect of TNT raises is shown by the following hand from a pairs competition.

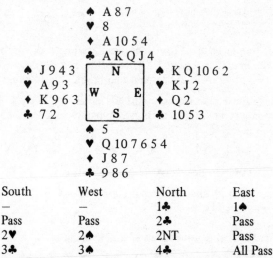

	♠ A 8 7	
	♥ 8	
	♦ A 10 5 4	
	♣ A K Q J 4	

♠ J 9 4 3		♠ K Q 10 6 2
♥ A 9 3	N	♥ K J 2
♦ K 9 6 3	W E	♦ Q 2
♣ 7 2	S	♣ 10 5 3

	♠ 5	
	♥ Q 10 7 6 5 4	
	♦ J 8 7	
	♣ 9 8 6	

South	West	North	East
—	—	1♣	1♠
Pass	Pass	2♣	Pass
2♥	2♠	2NT	Pass
3♣	3♠	4♣	All Pass

1♣ was strong, and South's first pass denied the values for a positive response. A trump lead might have beaten 4♣, but a spade lead did not.

Look at the auction from West's point of view, and consider your opinion of his part in it.

His decision to go to 3♠ is not bad, after all if the heart finesse is right, 3♠ is a make. What is bad, however, is the means of getting to 3♠. West's bidding has had no effect whatsoever on the exchange of information by North-South. In all probability they would have bid exactly the same way if he had remained silent throughout. If partner overcalls on thin values, 3♠ on the first round may look adventurous. Of course it entails some risk, but it is the lesser risk, for it is much more dangerous to bid 3♠ on the third round after the opponents have had four natural bids, and will have formed a good impression of their own values. Now they will know whether to double, bid on, or pass. What is more, consider the problems they will have after: 1♣ - 1♠ - Pass - 3♠. The contract of 3♠ hangs on a knife edge. From their point of view it could make or go two off, and they might have game on. They cannot hope to do the right thing all the time. If 3♠ is unprofitable it is bound to go unpunished some of the time provided it is bid immediately.

The essence of a TNT raise is that it is immediate, and reflects the full value of the hand. A responder who has made a limit bid is not expected to bid again. However, sometimes there may be good reason for flaunting this general principle. For example:

1♠	2♦	2♠	3♦
Pass	Pass	?	

The vulnerability and scoring may be such that responder will wish to push to 3♠ in spite of his partner's pass. But after a sequence such as:

1♥	1♠	3♥	3♠
Pass	Pass	?	

it is bad technique to press to 4♥, and be faced with the problem of what to do over 4♠. Partner has passed 3♠, and that is a decision which should be respected. He knows more about your hand than you do about his.

TNT raises must take into account the difficulty likely to be experienced by the opponents in finding their fit. A hand considered earlier illustrates the principles involved.

♠ K 10 7 6 5   ♥ 9   ♦ Q 4 3   ♣ J 8 5 4

1♣ (strong)	1♠	Pass	?

There are three possible course of action: a) 4♠, b) 3♠, or c) 3♠ with the intention of bidding 4♠ over 4♥.

a) If partner has fitting values even a hand as weak as:

♠ A 9 8 3 2   ♥ 10 4 3 2   ♦ K J 2   ♣ 7

could give excellent play for game. On balance however, 4♠ is intended as an advance sacrifice which might roll in on a lucky day.

b) Depending on the distribution of the heart suit, 3♠ may have the same pre-emptive effect as 4♠, and certainly stands a better chance of making.

c) This is an attempt to gain the best of both worlds. Although technically unsound, it is tempting to try it. There are two drawbacks. First, opener may double for take-out, the hearts may be bid on the right, and there may be no defence to 5♥ or even 6♥ when the suit could have been shut out by a raise to 4♠. Secondly, if opener bids 4♥ which is passed back to you, you cannot expect partner to have doubled on Q-10-x-x in hearts, just to prevent you from taking a phantom sacrifice. From his point of view the raise to 3♠ may have forced an error, and a double from his hand would guide the enemy back on the right track into five or six of a minor.

These are the issues involved. A player must be aware of the pros and cons for each line of action, and cultivate the art of being lucky.

One of the desirable side effects of TNT raises is that the opponents have problems. A great deal of heated discussion arose from:

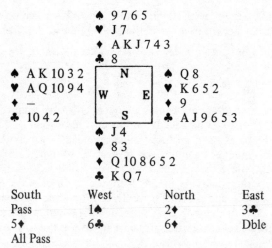

South	West	North	East
Pass	1♠	2♦	3♣
5♦	6♣	6♦	Dble
All Pass			

North maintained that he had to sacrifice since he had no defence. South argued that if 5♦ merely meant 'heads you win, tails we lose', then it was not a very smart bid; if the opponents had no losing options, 5♦ couldn't win. North countered by saying that he couldn't possibly judge his own values if 5♦ showed either nought or two defensive tricks against a club slam. South retorted that it was not for North to guess, that was the prerogative of the opponents; after all North had no defence to a grand slam, and his bid of 6♦ might push them into it. East-West bid and made 6♥ in the other room, but North-South came to no satisfactory conclusions.

It is neither possible nor desirable to formulate a rule of how many defensive tricks a TNT raise should or should not show. Unassuming cue-bids throw some light on this matter, but all that can be said for certain is that a TNT raise does not invite a continuation.

Take another more common sequence: 1♠ - 2♣ - 4♠. The bid of 4♠ means no more than, 'I think that it is in our interests to bid to this level'. Perhaps 4♠ is an advance sacrifice, perhaps it is making.

What is more likely is that the player who bids it will not know. But partner is not expected to emerge with a studious and well-considered bid of 5♠ if the opponents bid on. If he does bid 5♠ that is because he expects to make it. Similarly, if he doubles a continuation, that will be because he expects to beat it. One of the most foolish reasons for doubling the enemy is fear that partner will bid on if you do not double.

A very simple axiom emerges. After a TNT raise neither player is expected to bid again. Neither is barred from bidding again, but if he does so, it will be for a good reason, not because he had a vague feeling that something is expected of him. A forcing pass only exists when it is clearly understood by both players that their side holds the clear majority of the strength.

Once a basic discipline is established, it is possible to go on from there to define some sequences as more invitational than others. Consider:

| 1♣ | 1♠ | Pass | 4♠ |

and

| 1♠ | 2♣ | 2♠ | 3♣ |

In the first case 4♠ is bid before the opponents have found a fit, and may be stretched. In the second case the opponents have found a fit and made a limit bid, 3♣ causes them no inconvenience and they are unlikely to go far wrong in the subsequent auction. 4♣ instead of 3♣ might remove their trial bid mechanism, but either bid may help them to judge their fit. If 3♣ is an effort to stop them playing in 2♠, there are stronger ways of doing it, a competitive double and a competitive 2NT will be discussed later. 3♣ is no more than a club fit denying the ability to bid 4♣, and suggesting to partner that he should consider sacrificing against 4♠ if it is bid. If it is not, why bid it?

As a general guide: The more space taken from opponents who have not found a fit, the more pre-emptive the nature of the bid, and the less high cards which can be relied on. Conversely, a bid which takes no bidding space from the opponents must be of serious intent, either to buy the contract or to find a profitable sacrifice.

PART II

Conventions in Competition

Chapter 10
The Unassuming Cue-Bid

You are playing in a local pairs event with a player whose card play is good, but whose bidding is somewhat lacking in refinement. Third in hand you open 1♥ on:

♠ A 7   ♥ K Q 10 7 4   ♦ K Q 3   ♣ J 9 2

the next hand overcalls 1♠, and partner bids 2♠. Do not make the mistake of supposing that this is an unassuming cue-bid.

Partner's bidding is such that he has difficulty in recognising a common or garden cue-bid, and it is wildly improbable that he has ever heard of an unassuming cue-bid. The only thing you can be sure of is that partner does not propose playing in 2♠, although come to think of it, it would be unwise to totally overlook that possibility. Is it possible that he is looking for another suit with a view to playing five of a minor? Fortunately you have no minor to bid. Which does he most want to hear about, rebiddable hearts or a spade stop? That you have no way of guessing. In a well ordered world 3♠ would no doubt show both. But this is by no means a well ordered world, 3♠ will provoke 3NT as sure as night follows day. So, the choice seems to be 2NT, 3♥, 3♠, 3NT or 4♥. Would 2NT or 3♥ be forcing when partner has already passed? There is no reason why they should be, but since he won't know either, he will probably bid again. Is there any advantage in getting in the first bid in no-trumps? If his spade holding is as good as K-x or Q-x-x it won't much matter who plays no-trumps, but if he has Q-x, J-x-x or 10-x-x-x in spades there is considerable advantage in hogging the no-trump contract.

All things being considered 2NT must be the best choice. This will give him the chance to bid 3♥ which can be raised to 4♥. If he passes 2NT, you may as well take your chances there as anywhere else.

In fact he raises cheerfully to 3NT, the king of spades is led and all is revealed:

♠ J 10 4   ♥ A 9 5 4   ♦ 8 7 6 4   ♣ A Q

Your problem now is to make as many trick in no-trumps as every sane pair is making in 4♥. Needless to say you do not succeed in this task, and in due course you record your average minus.

The object in quoting this hand is to show the futility of playing the cue-bid of the opponent's overcall as a general purpose force. This cue-bid creates more problems than it solves unless there is a clear understanding how opener should react. If it is agreed that the cue-bid shows a full value raise to the three level of opener's suit, opener can still rebid two or three no-trumps, or introduce another suit as a game try. The loss of a general purpose force is slight or non existent, for a simple change of suit will fulfil the same function more economically and efficiently; the gain of unassuming cue-bids is huge and far reaching.

TNT raises against opponents who have not located their fit are lethal weapons. But what is partner expected to do if he is going to be raised to three or four of a major on five trumps to the king, a singleton and a queen? The answer is that he is not expected to do anything, if he were expected to do something you would have produced an unassuming cue-bid.

1♦ - 1♠ - Pass - 3♠   Partner is not invited to continue, he does so at his own risk if he has considerable reserves of strength.

1♦ - 1♠ - Pass - 3♦   This is a game invitation in spades.

Similarly by the opening side:

1♥ - 2♣ - 3♥   Pre-emptive, who knows, they may have a spade fit.

1♥ - 2♣ - 3♣   Game invitation, showing a high card raise to 3♥.

These cue-bids must be used whenever partner's opinion is being sought. Do not assume though, that it is always desirable to bring partner in on the act. In bridge, accuracy for its own sake is a very poor precept. It is well known that either:

♠ K 10 7 6   ♥ 8 5 2   ♦ A 9 4 3 2   ♣ 8

or

♠ K 10   ♥ A Q 8 5   ♦ A J 10 4   ♣ Q J 8

is a raise of a weak two spades to game. Any distinguishing between the two hands can be safely entrusted to the opposition. Partner's hand is clearly defined, and he is not expected to bid again.

A similar situation occurs with the direct raises to game in competition. After: 1♥ - 2♣ - 4♥ in a strong club system, responder may have either:

♠ 3   ♥ K J 8 7 6 4   ♦ Q 4   ♣ 10 7 6 3

or

♠ K J 9 3   ♥ K Q 7 4   ♦ Q 4   ♣ K 10 6

If fourth hand is contemplating a bid of 4♠ he may be interested to know which type of hand is on his right, but partner is unlikely to be concerned. If it is necessary in Acol to differentiate between these two responding hands for the purposes of a slam, that may be one of the attendant evils of opening bids which describe a wide range of hands. Certainly there is no merit in describing the difference for the benefit of the opposition.

For the opening side the cue-bid is most vital when the raise is to the three level, opener must know if he is being invited to bid game.

The unassuming cue-bid is particularly helpful to the defending side since there is a constant pressure to sacrifice.

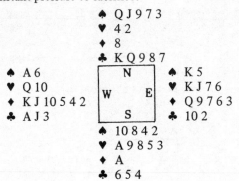

```
                    ♠ Q J 9 7 3
                    ♥ 4 2
                    ♦ 8
                    ♣ K Q 9 8 7
    ♠ A 6                              ♠ K 5
    ♥ Q 10            N                ♥ K J 7 6
    ♦ K J 10 5 4 2  W   E             ♦ Q 9 7 6 3
    ♣ A J 3            S               ♣ 10 2
                    ♠ 10 8 4 2
                    ♥ A 9 8 5 3
                    ♦ A
                    ♣ 6 5 4
```

The actual bidding was:

South	West	North	East
Pass	1♦	1♠	3♦
4♠	5♦	5♠	Pass
Pass	Dble	All Pass	

The fault lies in the bid of 4♠. It is all too likely that partner will press on to 5♠ with a hand which is stronger offensively than defensively. The correct bid on the South hand is 4♦. This is the nearest one can expect to get to a high card raise to 4♠ after this bidding. The message is that as far as South can judge, the hand belongs to his side, partner should not sacrifice against 5♦. The fact that the hand contains the ace of diamonds is entirely coincidental, the cue-bid of 4♦ does not relate to the holding in the suit.

There is no difficulty in recognising an unassuming cue-bid. What partner must remember is that raises by the defending side are primarily defensive and obstructive.

1♠ - 2♥ - Pass - 3♥   3♥ may be one off, but presumably in a good cause.

1♦ - 1♠ - Dble (neg) - 3♠   If 3♠ is on a losing finesse, it should still show a profit, partner is not being asked to bid one more.

The unassuming cue-bid can be made at different levels.

After the sequence: 1♣ - 1♠ - Pass any raise in spades will be understood as pre-emptive. This leaves 2♣, 3♣, 4♣ as strong bids. The bid of 2♣ is the traditional move on a strong hand. The inherent disadvantage of the bid of 2♣, is that it allows opener to bid again very cheaply, and he may find a fit in a red suit. A hand from match play showed this very vividly.

At love all the bidding was: 1♣ - 1♠ - Pass and fourth hand held:

♠ A 10 4 2   ♥ J 2   ♦ Q 9 3   ♣ A 10 8 3

2♣ was the bid chosen, impeccable according to accepted precepts. The full bidding was:

South	West	North	East
–	1♣	1♠	Pass
2♣	2♥	2♠	4♥
4♠	5♥	Pass	Pass
Dble	All Pass		

```
                    ♠ K Q J 8 7 6
                    ♥ 6 4
                    ♦ K J 7
                    ♣ 9 4
  ♠ 3            ┌─────────┐      ♠ 9 5
  ♥ K Q 9 3      │    N    │      ♥ A 10 8 7 5
  ♦ A 4          │ W     E │      ♦ 10 8 6 5 2
  ♣ K Q J 7 6 2  │    S    │      ♣ 5
                 └─────────┘
                    ♠ A 10 4 2
                    ♥ J 2
                    ♦ Q 9 3
                    ♣ A 10 8 3
```

North led the king of spades. Neither North nor South saw the urgency to switch to diamonds, and all of dummy's losing diamonds disappeared on the clubs. 5♥ doubled and made.

With a high card raise to 3♠ fourth hand will bid 3♣. A high card raise to 4♠ will bid 4♣. On the hand above South would bid 3♣. West might still bid 3♥, but it is not easy for him. North would have no reason for accepting game, and nine tricks would be made in spades.

The proposed use of the bid of 2♣ bears a certain resemblance to the competitive double, and will be discussed later after competitive doubles have been introduced.

Unlike TNT raises where partner is not expected to bid on, these unassuming cue-bids invite partner's co-operation, either to double or bid on.

1♦	1♠	Dble (neg)	3♦
Dble	3♠	4♦	?

Having described the hand once, there is no necessity to bid the same values again. Although partner has declined the opportunity to bid game freely, he might be prepared to bid one more now, or he might be pleased to double. On the other hand his bid of 3♠ might have been no more than an attempt to shut out the heart suit, and he will pass allowing the opponents to play a contract which they cannot be sure is the right one.

When the defending side cue-bids, it will be at a level appropriate to the strength of the raise. For example:

1♠ - 2♦ - Pass - 3♦ or 4♦   Defensive.

1♠ - 2♦ - Pass - 3♠ or 4♠ or 2♠   Full strength raises in diamonds.

The message behind each of these bids is clear once the principles are understood. 3♠ is a raise to 4♦ which invites game in no-trumps or diamonds, it is based on high cards, and partner should think twice about bidding over 4♠ from the opposition unless he expects to make it. 4♠ is a strong raise to game in diamonds; at favourable vulnerability a raise to 5♦ might be an advance sacrifice on a weak distributional hand. The bid of 2♠ will be discussed in more detail later, but it is clear from first principles that responder is prepared to hear a rebid of 2NT or 3NT if the overcaller can stop the spades, and expects a rebid of 3♦ on a minimum hand.

The jump cue-bid by the defending side has the aim of preventing the opener from bidding again too cheaply. The argument loses its force when it is opener's partner who is considering a cue-bid. With the defensive strength associated with an opening bid added to the high card strength for a raise to the three level, there will normally be no worries about letting the enemy in too cheaply. After: 1♥ - 1♠ or 1♥ - 2♣ responder will cue-bid in the opponent's suit to show a high card raise to at least the three level. As opposed to the pre-emptive raise of 1♥ - any - 3♥, 1♥ - 1♠ - 2♠ allows maximum game investigation. Opener can bid 2NT, 3♣, 3♦ as game tries, or bid the game direct. 3♥ shows a minimum opening bid, and responder will only raise if he was going to game anyway.

The jump cue-bid by the opening side is therefore an idle bid, and can be used as a splinter bid showing slam interest and a singleton or void in the enemy suit. A repeat cue-bid would show no losers, void or singleton ace.

Chapter 11
Intervention by Fourth Hand

In the previous three chapters there has been a gradual shift of emphasis away from pure theory towards conventional applications. Lurking in the mind of most average players and many experts is the nagging suspicion that modern bidding is cluttered up with too much conventional gadgetry. Conventional gimmickry justifies its own existence, and proliferates. It is not the intention of this book to burden bridge players with yet more incomprehensible memory work. What is needed is a cold appraisal of accepted bidding practice in the light of total distribution and total number of tricks. That is the object of the ensuing chapters.

No doubt a logical starting point for a comprehensive guide to modern conventions in the competed auction might be the overcall. But this is not intended to be a comprehensive guide and TNT has little to add in this well trodden field except to endorse the modern tendency to get into the auction as frequently as possible in the hope of finding a fit and causing problems for the opposition. In all but top class bridge, players do not enter the bidding as often as they should. The Italians have led the world in this respect, and have shown that overcalling on distribution without too strong a regard for point count is a winning philosophy.

It is in the realm of intervention by the fourth hand that accepted theory is, to say the least, suspect. In a sequence such as:

1♣	Pass	1♠	?

if you have about a ten count and nine red cards, some sort of action is almost compulsory, particularly at favourable vulnerability. The fact that you do not expect partner to have much more than seven or eight points is totally unimportant. The prospect of a fit is what counts, and it is quite wrong to suppose that it is safer to stumble into the auction with thirteen points rather than ten.

For fourth hand to bid in a forcing situation such as this is sometimes referred to as 'coming in under the guns', and it is a widely held view that to do so requires a good hand. The idea being that one can always protect if the bidding dies at a low level. But why should the opponents be allowed a free run to find their own best contract, and when they have finished saying what they wish to, the defending side may then guess whether or not to protect?

The whole notion is ill conceived. It is like some crazy relay race where you take over the baton when the race is already won.

If you do adopt this philosophy of protection, the bids all too often fall out in such a way that protection is awkward:

| 1♣ | Pass | 1♠ | Pass |
| 1NT | Pass | Pass | ? |

Now you must protect a non-fit sequence where the opponents have defined their strength.

| 1♣ | Pass | 1♠ | Pass |
| 2♠ | Pass | Pass | ? |

Protection is at the three level.

| 1♣ | Pass | 1♠ | Pass |
| 2♣ | Pass | 3♣ | ? |

It is quite likely that both sides have a nine card fit, but it would be dangerous to come in now. The opportunity is lost.

Intervention by fourth hand should not be assumed to show strong values. The opening side have already laid claim to half the honour strength, or thereabouts, and this acts as a safety factor. Partner should not be any more excited by a bid after the sequence:

| 1♣ | Pass | 1♠ |

than he would be by protection after the sequence:

| 1♣ | Pass | 1♠ | Pass |
| 2♣ | Pass | Pass | |

Before deciding the best way of getting into the auction after 1♣ - Pass - 1♠, consider:

♠ K 10 4   ♥ A J 8 7 3   ♦ Q 9 7 2   ♣ 3

and

♠ 3   ♥ A J 8 7 3   ♦ Q 9 7 2   ♣ K 10 4

In the first case the cards are more likely to be lying favourably for your side; if you have seventeen points between you, they may well be the equivalent of the opposing twenty-three, and it is very much in your interests to enliven the proceedings. When the opponents are stronger than twenty-three, and they have some prospect of game, their game contract will fail more often when you have the first hand. Moreover, if you can harass them into choosing the second best game, it is on the first hand that their error is more likely to be costly.

Once partner is converted into realising that you do not hold the best hand at the table when you come in after: 1♣ - Pass - 1♠, there are two further, but much less important risks in bidding on an average shapely hand. You may have no eight-card fit; your eight-card fit is in a suit already bid by the opponents, and you are unable to locate the fit. In either case you pay dearly for your temerity in bidding without the playing strength that partner used to think you had in this situation. Consider the hand:

♠ A J 8 3   ♥ 3   ♦ K 10 4 3   ♣ Q 9 7 3

and the bidding is 1♥ - Pass - 1♠ - ?

The majors are breaking badly, and the cards seem well placed. It looks a good moment to stir things up. That there is no eight-card fit is a risk one should be prepared to take, but what would be unbearable is that partner should pay heavily for the privilege of playing a seven-card minor fit when there is an eight-card spade fit, with 2♠ a possible make your way. Any system of competing on this type of weak distributional hand must take into account the possibility of playing in the suit bid by the right hand opponent.

Given the original sequence of 1♣ - Pass - 1♠ there are three possible ways of competing cheaply. Neither double, 1NT, nor 2♣ would be interpreted as natural bids. They are all available to describe different types of hands. Before assigning some arbitrary interpretation to each of these bids, it is wise to consider how each bid affects the opponents' bidding.

Double causes no distress whatsoever. In fact it gives opener two extra bids, pass and redouble. A good partnership will no doubt have laid down general principles as to how to take advantage of such extra options. 1NT deprives opener of one rebid only, 1NT itself; he should have not much difficulty in working out that double would be a good replacement. 2♣ is the intervention which nibbles insidiously at the opponents' bidding structure, depriving them of the 1NT rebid and all its attendant gadgetry such as Crowhurst. Opponents who describe a wide range of hands through the narrow channel of the 1NT rebid should have this passage blocked for them as often as possible, and however the three bids are to be used, 2♣ must describe the most frequent type of hand.

It would be possible to harness these three bids to show hands of varying strength, or various respective lengths in the red suits. But the painting of accurate pictures of honour strength and distribution is totally misguided if the opponents are merely going to pursue their own constructive bidding thankful for the information of how to play the hand. The intervention need be only as specifically defined as is necessary to wriggle out of a heavy penalty when challenged. The best policy is to stake out an option on three suits, the two unbid suits, and the suit bid by right hand opponent, and the following is one way of doing it.

After 1♣ - Pass - 1♠ - Double shows five spades, or a good four-card spade suit, and at least three cards in each unbid suit.

1NT shows four spades, and three cards at least in each unbid suit.

2♣ is general take-out for the red suits, nothing else specified.

At first sight it may appear strange to use the three available bids in this way. If the opponents start looking for a penalty it would seem wiser to use the bids to show different strengths in the unbid suits. This is not the case. The business of sorting out which is the better of the unbid suits comes only after the opponents have started on the warpath.

1♣ - Pass - 1♠ - 2♣

Although some opponents may double 2♣ out of pique, the double will be used most astutely as the first move towards extracting a penalty. The next hand should make any bid which is obvious. There are also two extra bids available, pass and redouble. Redouble is reserved to describe the awkward hand which contains one card more in the higher ranking suit. Redouble on either:

♠ Q 8 6 5   ♥ Q 4 2   ♦ 10 2   ♣ J 7 4 2

or

♠ J 4 3   ♥ 10 6 5 4   ♦ Q 3 2   ♣ K 8 3

Partner has probably chosen the wrong moment to compete, but he may still be able to avoid the double in 2♦ , and if he has made a bad bid with five diamonds and only three hearts, he will know that 2♦ is the better resting place. Pass will be the normal course of action with no particular preference, but Pass is better defined as 'nothing to say'. With three hearts and a singleton diamond it might be better tactics to wait for 2♦ to be doubled before bidding 2♥. If you pass, and 2♣ doubled runs back to partner who redoubles, his redouble has more or less the same meaning as your would. He has a slight preference for the higher ranking suit, either a card more in a weaker suit, or suits of the same length with the higher ranking being appreciably stronger. This apparent double safety device is useful to avoid the necessity of responder putting a delicate toe on 2♦ if he has three diamonds and two hearts or four small diamonds and three hearts to an honour. It also makes it much safer for fourth hand to come in with a 6-4 in the reds either way round. Let us look at the two sample hands to see how the system works.

♠ K 8 4   ♥ K Q 9 7 6   ♦ A J 8   ♣ 6 4

and

♠ 6   ♥ A Q 5 3   ♦ K J 7 6 5 2   ♣ 8 3

After 1♣ - Pass - 1♠ both of these hands would like to enter the auction. To bid two of the better red suit has obvious disadvantages. On the first hand there is no reason at all why partner should run to 3♦ if he has a respectable five-card diamond suit, or a weak six-card suit. If 2♣ is doubled and partner volunteers 2♦ this is likely to be the best spot, he would not bid it with four diamonds and three hearts. If he passes you know that you must take your chances in 2♥, confident that you have not missed a better diamond fit. On the second hand it appears dangerous to announce a red two suiter, but with three hearts and two diamonds partner redoubles 2♣, if he volunteers 2♥ it is probably the best strain. The drawback of bidding a safe 2♦ on this hand is that partner may have king to four or five hearts, and the fit is never discovered.

It can be seen that opponents assist by doubling 2♣, as is the case with doubles of most conventional bids. It may be better for opener to pass and force the next hand to choose between the red suits. But opener is caught on the horns of a dilemma, for passing relinquishes the initiative and renders his double on the next round ambiguous.

<h2 style="text-align:center">1♣ - Pass - 1♠ - 1NT</h2>

1NT by the defending side is a playable contract doubled, but not redoubled. There is no reason why 1NT doubled should not make on a combined nineteen count with the black suits held over the bids. If opener doubles 1NT and partner passes, this means that he wishes to play there, redouble is for take-out and can be used to show one card more in the higher ranking suit. It is quite likely that 1NT will be bid on a 4-3-5-1 or 4-5-3-1 shape, and redouble avoids choosing a 4-3 fit when there is a 5-3 fit available.

<h2 style="text-align:center">1♣ - Pass - 1♠ - Dble</h2>

1♠ redoubled by the enemy is an acceptable gamble. 1NT by the defending side is playable doubled but not redoubled, to bid 1NT and redouble can be used to show one card preference for the higher ranking suit.

The opponents bid other suits

The sequence 1♣ - Pass - 1♠ has been taken as the starting point for discussion of any action by fourth hand. The essential conclusion is that players should compete more freely in this position, and any serious partnership should discuss the difference between the three possible ways of entering the auction. Ideally conventions should be simple, logical, and easily remembered. Unfortunately with fourth hand intervention the logic of the situation changes according to the two suits bid by the opponents. Thus if the opening bid is 1♦ or 1♥ and the response is 1♠ there are only two ways of entering the auction on minimum values because the cue-bid of LHO's suit forces the bidding up to the three level in clubs. Therefore double shows a three suiter with at least four cards in spades, 1NT is take-out for the other two suits.

The situation changes yet again if the response is not 1♠. After an opening bid of 1♣ or 1♦ and a response of 1♥ the most likely successful contract for the defending side is in spades since the opponents can be outbid at the same level, but there will be many hands where partner is not prepared to go to 2♠, therefore double should be reserved for two suited take-out. With five or six spades and four of the unbid minor fourth hand might double, or might prefer to bid 1♠; a bid of 1NT would logically and safely show five or six of the unbid minor and four spades.

The opening bid of 1♣ and the response of 1♦ introduces a new idea. Clearly the safest way of entering the auction on minimum values is to double, for neither major need be bid above the one level on an unsuitable hand, but the bids of 1NT, 2♣, and 2♦ are available for interpretation. Each bid forces the bidding to the same level, and therefore shows the same values, the suggestion is that the lowest bid shows preference for the cheaper unbid suit, the next bid shows preference for the other suit, and the third bid shows even length.

Stronger hands

So far intervention has been no more serious than an immediate overcall. Of course if partner has five or six cards in one of the unbid suits he will be delighted to jump the bidding, but he does not expect a strong hand and will not become excited if he holds a flattish ten count. The question arises, therefore, as to what fourth hand should do with a strong two-suiter.

Imagine: 1♦ - Pass - 1♠ - ? and you hold:

♠ A 6   ♥ K Q J 4   ♦ 6   ♣ A J 10 7 4 3

or

♠ K 9   ♥ K Q 9 7 6 5   ♦ 9   ♣ A Q 10 6

or

♠ 6 5   ♥ A K 8 7 2   ♦ 5   ♣ K Q J 10 5

In each case, partner does not need much to make it worth while bidding to the four or five level, either to make or to sacrifice, and these are ordinary everyday hands. With something more exotic such as:

♠ 7 4   ♥ K Q J 9 5   ♦ −   ♣ K Q 10 8 4 3

it could be a mistake to go beyond the three level if partner has only four cards in your suits, but equally well it could be right to go to the six or seven level if he has a lot of clubs and hearts.

What is needed is a means of entering the auction which partner is expected to treat seriously. It must also cater for 6-4 hands whenever possible, for a natural bid in clubs on:

♠ A 4   ♥ K Q J 7   ♦ 8   ♣ A J 10 7 6 2

can lead to a missed 5-4 or 6-4 heart fit.

Let us study a typical sequence from first principles: 1♥ - Pass - 2♣ - ?

A double is the cheapest means of entering the auction, and will show the weakest type of hand.

2♦ and 2♠ must be reserved for natural bids but 2♥ is available for conventional interpretation. Since partner is not obliged to go beyond 2♠ with an unsuitable hand, there is no reason to assume that a bid of 2♥ should guarantee stronger values than a natural intervention of 2♠ would show. Double has already been set aside to show suits of more or less equal length, therefore 2♥ should show a bid of 2♠ with support for the unbid suit, and it follows that 2♥ invites correction to 3♦ whereas 2♠ does not.

2NT and 3♣ are strong bids forcing partner to the three level, and should show at least a good five loser hand. 2NT will show preference for the cheaper suit, diamonds; and 3♣, preference for spades. This makes it safer to come in on a 6-4 hand. With a 5-5 hand either double, or show which is the stronger suit by 2NT or 3♣.

A hand from play with the bidding as it occurred throws an interesting light on these proposed methods.

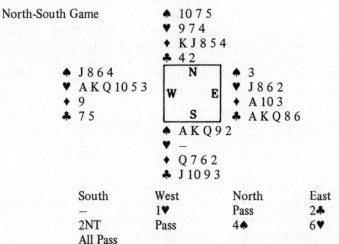

North-South Game

```
              ♠ 10 7 5
              ♥ 9 7 4
              ♦ K J 8 5 4
              ♣ 4 2
♠ J 8 6 4        N        ♠ 3
♥ A K Q 10 5 3            ♥ J 8 6 2
♦ 9         W       E    ♦ A 10 3
♣ 7 5            S        ♣ A K Q 8 6
              ♠ A K Q 9 2
              ♥ —
              ♦ Q 7 6 2
              ♣ J 10 9 3
```

South	West	North	East
—	1♥	Pass	2♣
2NT	Pass	4♠	6♥
All Pass			

2NT —   The hand is not strong enough, and at this vulnerability the bid is even more dangerous. This is a tailor-made bid of 2♥.

4♠ —   Ill judged. Although partner is weak for his bid, there is nothing wrong with his spade suit, yet the hand is likely to fall apart on repeated heart forces.

6♥ —   Responder was able to draw the correct inference that his partner had a weak hand with a good heart suit. However well thought out your defensive methods may be, there will always be occasions when it would have been better to be silent.

If South bids 2♥ and the next hand passes, at this vulnerability North does not want to know, and will bid a quiet 2♠. At favourable vulnerability he would consider a bid of 5♦ which might give the opponents a bit of bother.

Conventional Interference by Fourth Hand				
Opponents bid	Weak bids		Fairly strong bids	Strong bids
	3 suiter	2 suiter		
1♣ 1♠	Dble, 1NT	2♣		2♠, 2NT, 3♣
1♦ 1♠	Dble	1NT	2♦	2♠, 2NT
1♥ 1♠	Dble	1NT		2♥, 2♠, 2NT
1♣ 1♥		Dble	1NT, 2♣; 2♥	2NT, 3♣
1♦ 1♥		Dble	1NT; 2♦, 2♥	2NT
1♣ 1♦		Dble	1NT, 2♣, 2♦	2NT, 3♣, 3♦
1♦ 2♣		Dble, 2♦		2NT, 3♣, 3♦
1♥ 2♣		Dble	2♥	2NT, 3♣
1♥ 2♦		Dble	2♥	2NT
1♠ 2♣		Dble		2♠, 2NT, 3♣
1♠ 2♦		Dble		2♠, 2NT
1♠ 2♥		Dble		2♠, 2NT

It is intended that these bids should be conventionalised common sense, and not rote learning which may be forgotten. Nevertheless there are guiding principles to avoid slips in memory.

1   Three suiters are only shown when the response is 1♠, the defending side must not be excluded when opener has a singleton spade and responder has four to a minor honour.

2   The strength of the hand is dictated by the vulnerability and the level to which partner is forced to bid.

3   When there is a choice of two bids to show the same strength hand the lower bid shows preference for the cheaper suit.

4   With three bids available, the cheapest bid shows a better holding in the cheaper suit, the next bid preference for the other suit, and the third bid even length.

Chapter 12
Competitive Doubles

What sort of hand should a player hold to double for penalties in the sequence:

1♦	Pass	1♥	1♠
2♣	2♠	?	

The ingredients for the ideal hand would be: good trumps, no obvious fit for partner's suit, the balance of the points, but not a hand strong enough to make 3NT. A hand to meet these requirements was dealt in a local team of four match:

♠ K J 9 5　♥ A J 8 3　♦ 10 2　♣ 9 5 4

The player doubled, but failed to defeat the contract. The full deal was:

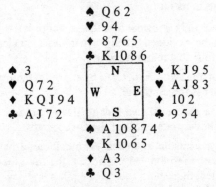

```
                    ♠ Q 6 2
                    ♥ 9 4
                    ♦ 8 7 6 5
                    ♣ K 10 8 6
     ♠ 3               N          ♠ K J 9 5
     ♥ Q 7 2                      ♥ A J 8 3
     ♦ K Q J 9 4    W    E        ♦ 10 2
     ♣ A J 7 2         S          ♣ 9 5 4
                    ♠ A 10 8 7 4
                    ♥ K 10 6 5
                    ♦ A 3
                    ♣ Q 3
```

2♠ by South cannot be defeated on best play, neither can 2NT by East. If either the East or West hand is strengthened sufficiently to ensure beating 2♠ there is a danger that 3NT will be a make for East-West. For instance, if the king and ace of diamonds are exchanged, 2♠ is beaten by one trick, but East can make nine tricks in no-trumps.

Even with an almost ideal hand the penalty double of 2♠ is a losing proposition, a fact supported by TNT theory. On the hand in question East should bid 2NT. The double should be employed to describe a different type of hand, a hand which has sufficient extra values to compete, but no satisfactory natural bid.

With:

♠ 7 3   ♥ Q 9 6 4 3 2   ♦ A 10   ♣ K 8 3
or
♠ 8 3   ♥ A Q 10 4 2   ♦ 8 5 3   ♣ K 9 8

East has every reason to suppose that his side can do better than allow the opponents to play 2♠, but either 3♣, 3♦, or 3♥ could prove to be the wrong choice. The double, which is defined as competitive, asks partner to choose.

From the other side of the table the double conveys the same message:

1♦	Pass	1♥	1♠
2♣	2♠	Pass	Pass
?			

Now it is opener who has extra values, and he is asking his partner to support a minor or rebid hearts.

This is the first of several different types of competitive double, and the rule is:

A DOUBLE BY THE OPENING SIDE IS COMPETITIVE WHEN THE OPPONENTS HAVE BID VOLUNTARILY AND FOUND A FIT AT THE TWO LEVEL.

This rule should apply whether the fit is specifically announced, as in:

1♦	1♥	1♠	2♥
Dble			

or whether it is tacitly understood:

1♠	1NT	Pass	2♦
Dble			

or:

1♠	Dble	Pass	2♥
Dble			

In both of these last two sequences it can be assumed that the opponents know what they are doing, and have alighted in an eight-card fit. There may be occasions when opener would like his double to be for penalties, but the need for a take-out double will be far more pressing.

If penalty doubles are abandoned at the two level, it does not follow that the opponents will be able to bid with impunity. In the sequence:

1♦	1♥	1♠	2♥

if opener has a hand on which he would like to make a penalty double he must pass, but partner is still there, equally aware of the need to compete, and he may make a competitive double if he has anything in reserve. Opener can then pass for penalties.

It is important that the opponents have bid voluntarily. When one bid is made under duress, a double is no longer competitive:

1♠	Dble	Rdble	2♦
Dble			

1♥	1NT	Dble	2♦
Dble			

Neither of the 2♦ bids in these auctions were made voluntarily, instead they were attempts to get off the hook, and so the doubles are for penalties.

The precise meaning of the competitive double will vary according to the sequence and the suits involved. It is rarely difficult to work out the message intended. Some examples will illustrate the general principles.

1	1♣	1♥	2♦	2♥
	Dble			

Basically the double shows a desire to compete and no satisfactory natural bid. If opener had a four card spade suit in this sequence, there would be no good reason for not showing it when that is the most economical bid. Therefore the double suggests a minor suit contract. It is looking for preference to clubs or rebiddable diamonds. Either:

$$♠ A J 6 \quad ♥ 9 4 3 \quad ♦ Q 6 \quad ♣ A K J 8 6$$

or

$$♠ A Q \quad ♥ 9 4 3 \quad ♦ Q 6 \quad ♣ A Q 8 6 5 4$$

would be typical. To bid 3♦ and find partner taking the force in hearts with a five-card trump suit would be a mistake. Equally 3♣ would be wrong if partner has six or seven diamonds and a singleton club.

Note that the competitive double is exactly what the name suggests, a means of competing. It does not guarantee vast reserves of strength, merely sufficient extra values to warrant another bid.

2	1♦	1♥	1♠	2♥
	Dble			

Here there could be a fit in any one of three suits, spades, clubs or diamonds. Opener may be able to visualise a possible fit in all three suits if he holds:

$$♠ 9 6 3 \quad ♥ 7 \quad ♦ A Q J 4 3 \quad ♣ A Q 10 4$$

Opener may double with potential in only two suits, provided he can control the auction. For example,

$$♠ J 4 3 \quad ♥ A 8 3 \quad ♦ A K Q 4 3 \quad ♣ J 6$$

This hand will also double 2♥, partner will rebid spades if he can, he is also expected to bid a four-card club suit. If the double produces 3♣ from partner, this will be corrected to 3♦ in the firm expectation of finding three-card diamond support. He must have some cards somewhere.

Assume the auction starts the same way, but takes a slightly different twist:

1♦	1♥	1♠	2♥
Dble	Pass	2♠	Pass
3♣	Pass	?	

Now what is he up to? Clearly he did not want rebiddable spades, so he is doing something in the minors. What he is doing depends on the basic system being played. To double on the second round and bid clubs on the third round shows a different hand to simply bidding clubs on the second round. Playing Acol, 3♣ on the second round would be obvious on:

♠ 6   ♥ 4 3   ♦ A K 10 4 2   ♣ K Q J 10 2

or

♠ 6   ♥ A 4 3   ♦ A Q 9 4 3   ♣ K Q 10 2

therefore 3♣ on the third round could show either:

♠ 6   ♥ 4 3   ♦ A K 10 4 3 2   ♣ A Q 7 4

or

♠ 6   ♥ A 4   ♦ A Q 10 4 3 2   ♣ A J 7 4

Playing a strong club system the inference is even more vital. 3♣ will be bid on the second round with good clubs and possibly weak diamonds, a hand like:

♠ 6   ♥ A 4 3   ♦ K 6 5 2   ♣ A Q J 9 4

whereas 3♣ on the third round might show:

♠ 6   ♥ A 4 3   ♦ A Q J 9 4   ♣ K 6 5 2

A crucial distinction which allows an awkward hand to compete unambiguously.

3	1♥	1♠	Dble (neg)	2♠
	Dble			

Here is another example of how the meaning of the second double can vary according to the basic system. If 1♥ is Acol, opener would have no qualms about introducing a four-card club suit, and might well bid a four-card diamond suit, thereby showing five hearts. Playing canape, opener could have longer clubs or diamonds after the opening bid of 1♥. Either suit would be bid readily since the Sputnik double guarantees some values in the minors. It is the hand with a good heart suit which is not so easily described. Therefore double would suggest good hearts, five or six, and tolerance for the minors.

4	1♦	Pass	1♥	1♠
	2♥	2♠	Pass	Pass
	Dble			

A more complicated auction but the same principle applies. Opener is suggesting clubs or diamonds as an alternative to hearts, his hand might be:

♠ 8 3   ♥ A J 8   ♦ A K 9 4   ♣ K 10 9 3

2NT in a competitive auction

The meaning of the bid of 2NT has a bearing on the competitive double:

1♥	1♠	Pass	2♠
2NT			

No matter what system opener is playing, it cannot be intelligent to bid 2NT as a natural bid opposite a passed partner. The bid of 2NT is available for conventional use in conjunction with the competitive double.

1♦	1♥	1♠	2♥
2NT			

In Acol there is no reason why 2NT should not be a genuine game try showing 17-18 points. Neither 1♥ nor 2♥ shows a powerful hand, 3NT could easily be playable by the opening side. But if opener is limited to fifteen or sixteen points, the bid of 2NT changes its character, no-trumps becomes a means of competing which outranks the spade suit. Thus it is possible in a strong club system to bid no-trumps more freely without fear of being misunderstood. There are three general rules.

1 2NT is never natural in a competed auction opposite a passing partner.

2 2NT is not a game try unless partner has shown strong values, such as a response at the two level, or a redouble of a take-out double.

3 When partner has shown a limited hand and a good suit, 2NT guarantees a fit for his suit.

Three hands follow which show these ideas in action.

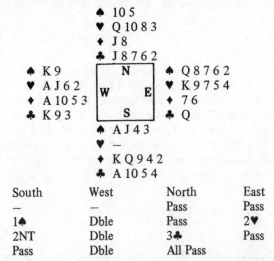

	♠ 10 5	
	♥ Q 10 8 3	
	♦ J 8	
	♣ J 8 7 6 2	
♠ K 9		♠ Q 8 7 6 2
♥ A J 6 2		♥ K 9 7 5 4
♦ A 10 5 3		♦ 7 6
♣ K 9 3		♣ Q
	♠ A J 4 3	
	♥ —	
	♦ K Q 9 4 2	
	♣ A 10 5 4	

South	West	North	East
—	—	Pass	Pass
1♠	Dble	Pass	2♥
2NT	Dble	3♣	Pass
Pass	Dble	All Pass	

The opening bid of 1♠ is clearly unsound in any system except the Blue Club. 2NT cannot be natural opposite a passing partner, and since a competitive double would have allowed preference to spades, the bid of 2NT asks for minors.

A trump lead would have held declarer to his contract, but a heart was chosen and declarer made an overtrick by playing on diamonds before touching trumps.

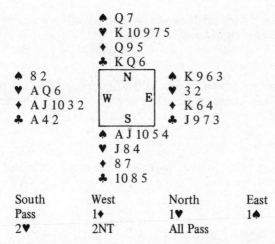

♠ Q 7
♥ K 10 9 7 5
♦ Q 9 5
♣ K Q 6

♠ 8 2
♥ A Q 6
♦ A J 10 3 2
♣ A 4 2

♠ K 9 6 3
♥ 3 2
♦ K 6 4
♣ J 9 7 3

♠ A J 10 5 4
♥ J 8 4
♦ 8 7
♣ 10 8 5

South	West	North	East
Pass	1♦	1♥	1♠
2♥	2NT	All Pass	

As has been shown in example 2 of the competitive doubles, West can compete over 2♥ with a double and still keep the auction under control. 2NT is a natural bid used as a means of outranking hearts in this case. Declarer is prepared to go one off. In fact on a heart lead he guessed the queen of diamonds and made eight tricks.

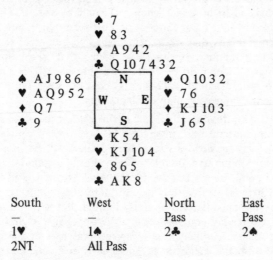

♠ 7
♥ 8 3
♦ A 9 4 2
♣ Q 10 7 4 3 2

♠ A J 9 8 6
♥ A Q 9 5 2
♦ Q 7
♣ 9

♠ Q 10 3 2
♥ 7 6
♦ K J 10 3
♣ J 6 5

♠ K 5 4
♥ K J 10 4
♦ 8 6 5
♣ A K 8

South	West	North	East
—	—	Pass	Pass
1♥	1♠	2♣	2♠
2NT	All Pass		

2♣ by the passed hand was competitive, promising no more than a good suit. 2NT promised a club fit. With a certain re-entry North took a good view in passing 2NT. A safer course of action might be to run to 3♣, but it should be noted that the opponents will be less ready to defend against 3♣. However 2NT bid and made when game in spades is on in the other direction is not a result to be criticised too severely.

When a competitive double and a competitive 2NT are both available there are shades of meaning attached to each.

1♥	1♠	Dble (neg)	2♣
Pass	Pass	?	

2NT cannot be natural in view of the failure to bid 1NT, therefore 2NT is conventional emphasising the minors, and a double would suggest secondary heart support.

1♠	Dble	Pass	2♥
?			

Double suggests rebiddable spades and tolerance for the minors and 2NT guarantees both minors.

1♥	1♠	Pass	2♠
?			

Double invites heart preference and 2NT is for the minors.

If there is any doubt whether 2NT is natural or conventional, it should always be treated as natural. Consider the following sequence:

1♥	1♠	1NT	2♠
Pass	Pass	2NT	

Since responder was proposing to make seven tricks in no-trumps, why let the enemy make eight in spades when 2NT could be one off. The bid of 2NT is natural, obviously the hand contains support for a minor, but disaster could ensue if opener thinks that he is being asked to volunteer some ridiculous three-card minor holding. It should be added that, since opener has not chosen to make a competitive double, this bid of 2NT is something of a hostage to fortune. It could make and it could be two off doubled. For sure it is a bid which requires favourable vulnerability.

The competitive doubles advocated in the last few pages are aggressive and often more appropriate non-vulnerable. In Acol opener can be caught in a competitive situation with a strong hand which will be more difficult to express if the competitive double merely shows a sound opening bid or response and good prospects of a fit. An Acol pair may well take the view that these light competitive doubles are more appropriate to a strong club system where the opening bid is strictly limited. But if it is understood that either hand will readily compete against the opponents' eight-card fit at the two level, it must be equally clearly agreed that part of the object of the exercise is to push the enemy to the three level and stand a better chance of defeating their contract. Partner is not expected to double them just because he has got his bid and they sounded reluctant. They may be quite prepared to advance to the three level, and will be delighted to be doubled into game.

Having issued a caution against what appears to be a very hazardous and ambitious philosophy of bidding, it is only right to emphasise that light competitive doubles are based on sound principles. Although in this last hand no competitive double is involved as such, the deal is a good example of TNT theory, the need to take a slight risk to disturb the opponents' eight-card fit at the two level, and the over-riding necessity to limit one's ambition, and not be too greedy.

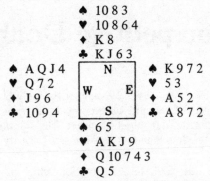

```
              ♠ 10 8 3
              ♥ 10 8 6 4
              ♦ K 8
              ♣ K J 6 3
  ♠ A Q J 4      N       ♠ K 9 7 2
  ♥ Q 7 2              ♥ 5 3
  ♦ J 9 6   W     E    ♦ A 5 2
  ♣ 10 9 4      S       ♣ A 8 7 2
              ♠ 6 5
              ♥ A K J 9
              ♦ Q 10 7 4 3
              ♣ Q 5
```

The hand occurred in a team of four match. East-West were vulnerable with West the dealer. Both Acol players opened the South cards with a bid of 1♥ fourth in hand. North made the obvious raise to 2♥, which at one table was passed out and just made. At the other table the bidding took a more interesting turn.

South	West	North	East
—	Pass	Pass	Pass
1♥	Pass	2♥	Dble
Pass	2♠	Pass	Pass
3♥	Pass	Pass	3♠
All Pass			

The double of 2♥ even at this vulnerability, is a justifiable risk. Since the hand has already passed partner will know that he must moderate his enthusiasm. The object of the exercise has been achieved when the opponents have been pushed to 3♥, which is bound to go one off. The bid of 3♠ is greedy and ill-disciplined. Par on the hand is strictly according to TNT and CTL. 2♥ can be made, and so can 2♠ since the defence cannot attack diamonds. As it turned out justice was served to some extent. Against 3♠ North chose to lead the king of diamonds. Not unnaturally declarer failed to read this lead for what it was, sustained a diamond ruff, and conceded 200.

Chapter 13
More Competitive Doubles

After the sequence: 1♠ - 2♥ - 2♠ - 3♥, opener has only one bid below the value of game, that is 3♠. Should partner read this as a game try or an attempt to buy the contract? It might be either. The solution is to abandon the penalty, and use the double in this position as a game try, leaving 3♠ as a competitive bid.

This introduces a little skill into a situation which is something of a lottery. What often happens when a sequence starts like this is that someone keeps bidding one more, usually in the protective position, for fear of letting the opponents play the hand. Nobody can guess whose hand it is, so everybody works on the principle that it can't be far wrong to play the hand. Such proceedings are usually closed when someone runs out of patience and doubles. Since the double is sometimes based mainly on a desire to stop partner continuing on the merry-go-round, much to everybody's surprise the contract makes. In that sort of game there is a strong case for fourth hand bidding 3♥ on a hand which is worth 4♥ in the almost certain knowledge that 3♥ will not be passed out. Alternatively phantom sacrifice follows phantom sacrifice until someone gets the winning double. A couple of months ago in a team of four match the bidding got to the five level on a hand that was passed out at the other table. The contract was doubled of course, but only went one down. Although the third in hand opener was a trifle shaded, no-one else was at fault, it was just a natural progression.

However, we are not concerned with what bidding is, but what it ought to be. If 3♠ is competitive in the auction above, what sort of hand is suitable? Here most average players would go wrong. You are directed to bid 3♠ on one of the following hands and pass the other. Which hand should pass?

♠ A Q 8 6   ♥ J 2   ♦ K J 7 6   A 10 2

or

♠ A Q 8 6 5 2   ♥ J 2   ♦ K J 7   ♣ K 2

The first thing to notice is that their trump suit is breaking evenly, and a doubleton in their suit is the worst possible holding either offensively or defensively. Three small hearts would be a better holding than two small. But if you are going to bid 3♠ on one of these hands, it should be the first not the second. The TNT on the first is much lower, and someone is going to buy the phantom. Of course it may be you, but it is odds on that someone can make something at the three level. On the second hand the TNT is a full two tricks more to your knowledge, quite apart from any concealed length anyone else might have. Those extra tricks are not coming your way. It is a racing certainty that the opponents can make 4♥, but they may not bid it. In all probability they will be quite pleased to buy the contract in 3♥. It is equally probable that they will push to 4♥ over 3♠, and be even more pleased with the result. One approach worth considering on this second hand is to pass 3♥ and sacrifice against 4♥ if it is bid voluntarily.

When opener decides to pass or bid 3♠, responder should respect the decision of a partner who is almost certainly in a better position to judge. After:

1♠	2♥	2♠	3♥
3♠	4♥	?	

or

1♠	2♥	2♠	3♥
3♠	Pass	Pass	4♥
Pass	Pass	?	

4♠ is only right if 3♠ was wrong.

Conversely:

1♠	2♥	2♠	3♥
Pass	Pass	?	

It might be right to bid 3♠, but it is taking a decision which does not belong to you. You made your decision on the first round.

A system which deprives one player of his right to exercise his judgment is not a good system. Responder should be allowed some say. But if he is going to regard:

1♠	2♥	2♠	3♥
Pass	Pass	?	

as forcing, which in practice is what often happens, then opener might just as well bid 4♠ on the second round. It saves time, and at least the opponents will not know what is going on.

To push or not? Most players would get the next one wrong, and complain, justly perhaps, of being fixed.

North-South are vulnerable, playing pairs against weak opponents, and the bidding goes:

South	West	North	East
–	1♠	Dble	2♠
3♣	3♠	?	

North holds:

♠ A 4   ♥ J 9 6 3   ♦ A 5 2   ♣ A K 5 3

The perennial problem. Who does the hand belong to? North chose 4♣, and not unexpectedly the bidding continued: 4♠ - Pass - Pass. Now what? North refrained from doubling and the full hand was:

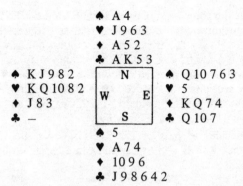

♠ A 4
♥ J 9 6 3
♦ A 5 2
♣ A K 5 3

♠ K J 9 8 2   ♠ Q 10 7 6 3
♥ K Q 10 8 2   ♥ 5
♦ J 8 3   ♦ K Q 7 4
♣ —   ♣ Q 10 7

♠ 5
♥ A 7 4
♦ 10 9 6
♣ J 9 8 6 4 2

—420 was an above average score in view of the many times —590 was recorded. The winning bid would probably have been 3NT by North, if East thought his hand was only worth 2♠, it is unlikely that he would have considered 4♠ over 3NT. The other possibility is to pass 3♠. If you cannot outbid them let have it as cheaply as possible.

Returning to the original sequence: 1♠ - 2♥ - 2♠ - 3♥, the competitive double was necessary because the opponents' suit ranked immediately below the opener's. In any other arrangement of the suits it will be possible for opener to introduce a new suit as a game try. For example: 1♠ - 2♣ - 2♠ - 3♣ opener can bid 3♦ or 3♥ as a game try. 3♦ or 3♥ may be a second suit which responder is free to raise, and if opener does not hold this suit he will convert to 4♠. Therefore there are four sequences only where double by opener is a game try:

1♠	2♥	2♠	3♥
1♥	2♦	2♥	3♦
1♦	2♣	3♦	4♣
1♣	1♠	3♣	3♠

In all other sequences a double retains its normal significance, penalties.

The problem is essentially unaltered if second hand makes a take-out double instead of a simple overcall, or a jump overcall in the last two examples. Therefore after:

| | 1♠ | Dble | 2♠ | 3♥ |

or

| | 1♦ | 3♣ | 3♦ | 4♣ etc. |

a double by opener is competitive.

Chapter 14
Competitive Doubles
by the Defending Side

Consider the two sequences:

1♠	2♦	3♣	?

and

1♥	1♠	2♦	?

If 3♣ or 2♦ is forcing it is exceedingly improbable that the fourth hand would wish to double for penalties. Such action would be premature, even if a hand occurred to justify a penalty double. In some variations of Sputnik responder's bid is non-forcing. If this is the case, a penalty double is a stronger possibility. But would it be wise? For fourth hand to apply the axe he must be strong enough to double the likely escape to 2♥ by opener, or is he to double 2♦, and then let the opponents play peacefully in 2♥, thereby helping them into a better contract? The penalty double in this situation is improbable and unwise. A far better idea is to use the double here as a conventional aid for solving awkward problems.

Fourth hand will have no problem with a fit for partner's suit, a TNT raise will be automatic. With a partial fit in partner's suit and values in the unbid suit, he will be unsure whether to try the remaining suit or raise partner. This is the type of hand to be shown by a double. After: 1♥ - 1♠ - 2♣ any of the following hands would be suitable for a double:

♠ J 10   ♥ A 10 2   ♦ K 9 8 7 6 2   ♣ 9 2

♠ 7 4 3   ♥ 2   ♦ K J 10 8 7 5   ♣ K 3 2

♠ K 3   ♥ 10 9 2   ♦ K Q J 5 2   ♣ 8 5 3

There is a very valuable negative inference if fourth hand introduces a new suit. He has no fit for his partner. The beauty of this is that the player who overcalled can judge the fit and TNT immediately by the probable length in two suits.

The fourth suit at minimum level denies a fit with partner. How strong the suit will be depends on the level at which it is introduced. After: 1♣ - 1♦ - 1♥ - 1♠ fourth hand need be no stronger than:

♠ K J 6 5 2   ♥ Q 10 7   ♦ J 7   ♣ 7 6 3

The opponents must be able to double 1♠, 1NT and 2♦ before they can extract a penalty, and the spade suit might be the controlling factor in the auction if partner is at home with three to an honour.

After: 1♦ - 1♠ - 2♣ - 2♥, the heart suit must be better since partner has been told not to run to 2♠ if 2♥ is doubled. But nevertheless there is the security of being able to run to 2♠ yourself if 2♥ is doubled and you have:

♠ 7 3 ♥ K J 7 4 3 2 ♦ 3 ♣ Q 10 4 2

If your suit is slightly better you will stick the double:

♠ 7 3 ♥ K J 10 9 4 2 ♦ 3 ♣ Q 10 4 2

and may even make the contract.

When the fourth suit is at the two level, and outranks partner's overcall, the eggs are all in one basket if the hand turns out to be a misfit. There is no escape from a penalty double.

After: 1♦ - 1♥ - 2♣, to bid 2♠ does not promise an enormous hand, but it does promise a good suit. It would be extremely dangerous to bid on less than:

♠ K Q 10 9 4 2 ♥ 3 ♦ 7 4 3 ♣ K 8 3

It would be acceptable to bid 2♠ on:

♠ K Q 9 4 3 2 ♥ 7 4 3 ♦ 3 ♣ K 8 3

with a run out to 3♥ if a double comes up. Note that a competitive double is no use on a hand like this. Is partner expected to bid 4♠ with a sound overcall and a doubleton honour in spades? Yet:

♠ A 8 ♥ A Q J 8 5 ♦ J 8 2 ♣ 10 5 4

gives a reasonable play for game in spades.

The strength of the fourth suit that would be introduced into a competitive auction is important because it is the limiting factor on the suit shown by a competitive double. No rules are advanced, but if the general principles are understood there should be no problem which cannot be solved by the exercise of a little common sense.

After the bidding: 1♣ - 1♦ - 1♥ you might make a competitive double on:

♠ A J 4 3 ♥ Q J 3 ♦ Q 3 ♣ 9 8 4 3

The TNT is very low, and someone might get caught here, but the double is eminently correct. Either 2♦ or 2♠ could be a very good contract. The spade suit is limited by the failure to bid it naturally.

After the same bidding, holding:

♠ J 9 4 3 2 ♥ K 4 ♦ 10 8 3 2 ♣ Q 2

double is still correct, asking partner to choose between 2♦ and 2♠. The fact that the opponents can probably make three or four more tricks on this occasion is entirely their problem, partner is expected to react the same way. If they bid to game and he doubles, he is an ass, all you have done is raise to 2♦ and shown a spade suit on the way.

After: 1♠ - 2♦ - 2♥ when the opponents have the values for an opening bid and a response at the two level, and they have an option on both the majors, the double should show serious intent. It would be futile exhibitionism to double on:

♠ K 8 4   ♥ J 9 3   ♦ Q 8   ♣ K J 8 4 2

urging the opponents to bid a thin game which will probably make now that you have told them how to play it. The double would show real values, preferably offensive and defensive. A hand such as:

♠ A 10 9 3   ♥ 3   ♦ Q 2   ♣ Q 10 8 7 3 2

is far more appropriate for stirring things up.

If the minor suits are reversed:

♠ A 10 9 3   ♥ 3   ♦ Q 10 8 7 3 2   ♣ Q 2

After the bidding: 1♠ - 2♣ - 2♥ the competitive double is even more valuable.

The competitive double can be a useful weapon, but it takes no space from the enemy. On the contrary it gives them the option of two extra bids, pass and redouble, which no doubt they will use as:

Pass   —   No extra length or strength

Redouble —   No particular fit, but extra values, shall we get at them?

The rest of the time they will simply proceed about their own business.

A hand given earlier was:

♠ 7 4 3   ♥ 2   ♦ K J 10 8 7 5   ♣ K 3 2

and double was recommended after: 1♥ - 1♠ - 2♣. Vulnerable this bid can be recommended for its sobriety, but non-vulnerable something a little more adventurous is called for. Or if the hand is strengthened to:

♠ J 4 3   ♥ 2   ♦ K J 10 8 7 5   ♣ K 3 2

or

♠ 7 4 3   ♥ 2   ♦ A J 10 8 7 5   ♣ K 3 2

there is a more aggressive bid than double.

Double is the immaculate bid which allows you to congratulate yourself on how well you have played in spite of the fact that you lost. If you wish to win at the game you bid 3♦ on this type of hand. Partner receives the message of moderate trump support, a good suit, and sufficient values to be keen to buy the contract, possibly against the balance of the points. This jump in a new suit when everybody is bidding always has the same meaning. What you are going to do is clear, you are going to play a spade or diamond contract at the three level, or possibly higher if partner fits very well. What they propose to do about it is their affair.

The competitive double where the opening side have bid two suits can occur in a slightly different guise. After:

| 1♥ | Pass | 1♠ | 2♣ |
| 2♠ | ? | | |

the opponents have found a fit and a competitive double will be useful more frequently than a penalty double. The announced fit is critical.

If the bidding were:

1♥	Pass	1♠	2♣
2♥	?		

the odds favour retaining the double for penalties, since the hand could be a hideous misfit, and the second player might be waiting in eager anticipation.

So far the competitive doubles by the defending side have followed when the opening side has shown two suits. The double has a similar connotation when the opening side has bid and raised a suit. There is, however, one important distinction. In all of the sequences where three suits were bid round the table, there was no way of telling whether the deal was yielding a good fit and a high TNT, or whether each player had a good suit facing a singleton and whoever bought the contract would be unlucky. But once one side has bid and raised a suit, it becomes a question of bargain offers if you get there quickly.

A classic example is the sequence: 1♥ - 2♦ - 2♥ - Dble. The defending side may have a fit in spades, clubs, or diamonds. The double is an attempt to stake out a claim to any of these suits. The perfect hand would be:

♠ K 10 6 4 3   ♥ 3   ♦ Q 4   ♣ K 9 7 6 4

partner is expected to bid three cards to an honour in either of responder's suits in preference to rebidding his own.

In this example responder has hopes of a fit in three suits. Such a hand will be rare. Usually it will be a question of making the best of a poor job on a hand which is less than ideal, but can control the bidding:

♠ A 9 8 3 2   ♥ 5 3 2   ♦ A 3   ♣ J 6 2

or

♠ A Q J 4   ♥ J 10 4 2   ♦ J 4 3   ♣ 8 2

If partner cannot show three spades to an honour, he will probably bid 3♣ and this can be converted to 3♦. The chances are that partner can scratch around and make eight or nine tricks.

In these last two examples responder had a weak five-card spade suit, not strong enough to be introduced in its own right, or a good four-card spade suit. In both case partner was expected to a bid a three-card spade suit to an honour. The spade suit acted as an anchor. Would it be possible to double without spades, holding clubs and diamonds? A hand such as:

♠ A 4 3   ♥ 2   ♦ 9 7 4   ♣ K J 8 7 6 3

It appears safe, because if partner bids 2♠, 3♣ will now show clubs and diamonds. This however, reckons without the opposition, who will be quite likely to bid 3♥ over the double, and with a good overcall and spade support partner is entitled to bid 3♠. In fact, whenever you have the spades and he has spade support and something in reserve that is precisely what you want him to do whether the opponents bid 3♥ or not. Therefore if fourth hand doubles without the requisite holding in the anchor suit, he must be correspondingly stronger. Incidentally if the bidding does continue:

1♥	2♦	2♥	Dble
3♥			

there is no necessity for the next player to volunteer 3♠ on a poor hand. Partner is still there in the protective position, and he is capable of bidding 3♠ to be converted to four of a minor without a fit. It is also possible that the mission is complete when the opponents have been pushed to the three level.

Another bid which should not be overlooked after: 1♥ - 2♦ - 2♥ is a competitive 2NT. The player may or may not stand a double, he will have diamond support and will not have a good four-card spade suit.

The sequence: 1♥ - 2♦ - 2♥ - Dble was referred to as classic since it contains ingredients typical of other auctions. An anchor suit, two other possible suits, and the availability of a competitive 2NT.

A more economical but less archetypal sequence would be: 1♦ - 2♣ - 2♦ - Dble. The doubler will be expected to hold values in the majors, the player who has overcalled will show a holding a three cards to an honour in a major at the two level, but will be wary of bidding spades at the three level if opener continues with 3♦. The doubler may or may not produce another bid.

♠ K J 6 5 3   ♥ A 3   ♦ 10 8 7 6   ♣ J 4

would feel confident of controlling the auction.

Many sequences will be less economical of space. The enemy will seldom play inverted major suit raises in order to let you come in and find your fit. The bidding will often be at the three level before you have had a chance to speak. Should the double be competitive at the three level? This is a purely arbitrary decision which has to be resolved by drawing a line somewhere. As good a place as anywhere is summed up in the definition: 'Always to 3♦, also to 3♥ if partner has not bid spades.'

1)	1♦ - 1♠ - 3♦ - Dble	competitive
2)	1♥ - 2♣ - 3♥ - Dble	competitive
3)	1♥ - 1♠ - 3♥ - Dble	penalties
4)	1♠ - 2♣ - 3♠ - Dble	penalties

In both 1) and 2) there is an unbid major at the three level. A competitive double for the minors in 3) with no spade fit is a waste of time, 3NT will do the job better. If you have a partial spade fit, you will have to put a delicate toe on 3♠ or pass. If you double competitively on 4) you just don't know when you're beat. Keep the axe sharp, and keep their spade raises honest.

Competitive doubles should be regarded as having some similarity with unassuming cue-bids, both should deter partner from sacrificing. In the sequence: 1♠ - 2♣ - 2♠ all raises in clubs by fourth hand are defensive, 3♠ shows a high card raise to 4♣ and promises defensive values, double also promises defensive values in the shape of length and strength in the red suits.

This sequence of 1♠ - 2♣ - 2♠ came up in a pairs tournament with the opening side vulnerable and the defending side non-vulnerable; fourth hand held:

♠ J 8 3   ♥ A 9 7 2   ♦ K Q 9 2   ♣ Q 4

and made the calculated underbid of 3♣ in the hope of trapping the opponents. The bidding proceeded: 4♠ - 5♣ - Dble and fourth hand was hoist on his own petard. Partner held:

♠ Q   ♥ 10 6 5 4 3   ♦ 8 6   ♣ A K J 9 3

and not unnaturally could not see much defence to 4♠. The competitive double would have allowed the defending side to bid to 4♥ in competition, and then defend, successfully, against 4♠.

Chapter 15
Consultative Doubles

In the previous three chapters suggestions have been made for abandoning penalty doubles in a variety of different bidding situations. For the purpose of easy reference these competitive doubles may be summarised as follows:

A double is not for penalties:
1   When the opening side doubles the opponents in an eight-card fit at the two level.
2   When both sides have a declared fit, and there is no bidding space for the opening side to make a game try.
3   When three suits have been bid round the table.
4   After an overcall and a raise of opener's suit.

The only feature these doubles have in common is that without partnership agreement to the contrary, such doubles would be understood as penalty doubles, but in practice it is more efficient to double asking partner to bid rather than asking him to pass.

These competitive doubles gain almost universal acceptance amongst expert tournament players regardless of their basic bidding system. Many players would go further, and add to this list, or extend the double to higher levels of bidding. For instance, it is standard practice to extend the fourth category.

| 1♦ | 2♣ | 3♦ | Dble |
| 1♦ | Dble | 3♦ | Dble |

Technically the double in the first sequence is classified as competitive, in the second sequence the final double is referred to as responsive, and is discussed later. But exactly the same principle applies, namely that a take-out double is more efficient than a penalty double.

In an ideal world doubles would either be for take-out or for penalties, and there would never be any partnership misunderstandings. Unfortunately ambiguous doubles exist, and will continue to do even if the theorists do far more research than has yet been attempted. Experts often refer to doubles as co-operative, biased towards penalties, suggesting take-out, optional, etc. Surprisingly often, though by no means always, their expert partners have the same intuitive interpretation of a complicated sequence which is terminated by an ambiguous double, and receive the message intended. In beginners' circles where the knowledge of ethics is rudimentary, the same shades of meaning are more effectively conveyed by doubling more loudly or more quickly. The average player is in a quandary, he knows that he cannot sit bolt upright in his chair, double in a loud voice and glower at his partner, neither can he wriggle and squirm and finally double with a rising intonation. But he does not have the intuition of the expert. Let us grasp this nettle of ambiguous doubles on behalf of the average player, and attempt to explain and classify.

Optional doubles, fittingly described as giving partner the option of making a mistake, should be expunged from the bridge players' vocabulary. A co-operative double, in the Bridge Players' Encyclopedia, is given the appropriately uncontroversial definition of 'a double which gives partner the option of passing for penalties or bidding further'. Let us use the term consultative, which was coined many years ago, to describe a means of extracting penalties from an overcall. The Colonel's double of an overcall was for penalties spelt with a capital P, and had to be left in with thirteen cards, an offender who removed such a double risked being cashiered from the regiment, spelt with a capital R.

The consultative double of an overcall is more subtle, it shows shortage in partner's suit, the balance of the points, and a trump holding of three to an honour or better. If opener has a suitable hand the overcall can be butchered on a defensive cross ruff, or dummy's trumps can be removed and declarer effectively plays the hand in no-trumps. Clearly opener does not leave the double with a singleton trump, that would be an unsuitable hand.

The consultative double is a penalty suggestion which partner is free to remove on an unsuitable hand.

Consider the following two sequences:

1♦	1♥	1♠	2♥
?			

and

1♦	1♥	1♠	4♥
Dble			

The double of 2♥ is competitive, in other words, take-out. The double of 4♥ is for penalties, but since the opponents are expecting to be doubled, responder should remove the double on an unsuitable hand, a hand short in points, long in spades, and with a diamond fit:

♠ Q 10 9 7 6 2   ♥ 3   ♦ K J 4 3   ♣ 4 2

A competitive double has become a consultative double at a higher level. Some players would say that the change takes place at the three level, or above the level of 3♥, others would argue that the change takes place at the four level; the only satisfactory answer, of course, is by partnership agreement.

1♦	1♥	1♠	3♥
Dble			

A majority of Acol players agree that this double is competitive, for the following reasons:

1   Opener may have a wide range of possible hands which can be more accurately described with the use of a competitive double than without it.

2   A bid of 4♣, even if it is not forcing, will be treated by partner as highly encouraging, and this may overstate the value of the hand.

Strong club players should be aware that competitive bidding theory, sketchy as it may be in certain areas, was largely evolved for use in conjunction with natural bidding. The two arguments stated above apply with less force to a club system, and it may be right for them to confine opener's competitive double to the two level.

Consultative doubles may occur in the following situations:

1   Above the agreed level of competitive and responsive doubles
2   Doubles of suits at the one level
3   After the second round of bidding
4   Under the suit bid
5   Doubles of pre-emptive overcalls

1 These have already been discussed, but as a further example, assume that responsive doubles are being played by the defending side up to and including 3♥, and consider the sequence: 1♣ - Dble - 4♣ - Dble. By agreement this is not competitive. There is a big club fit, and the TNT is high. The opponents will be delighted to be left to play 4♣ undoubled. What is good for them is not good for the defending side, fourth hand should strain to bid a firm confident four of a major, even if he doesn't feel confident. The double cannot be a trump stack, it shows defensive values and denies the ability to speculate in four of a major. If the partnership wishes to double here to show four cards in each major, that involves redefining the responsive double to include four of a minor.

2 What are the prospects of playing in a 5-1 trump fit at the two level when trumps are breaking badly? The Colonel's doubles presuppose that it is a good idea. When an opponent's non-vulnerable overcall at the one level is doubled for penalties, the defending side must make eight tricks to show a profit. The Colonel often shows a singular lack of appreciation of the niceties of the scoring.

In a sequence such as:

1♦	Dble	Rdble	Pass
Pass	1♠	Dble	

the double should be considered as consultative, partner is not commanded to pass with a singleton, he will be ill-advised to do so.

This sequence came up in a Gold Cup match, and opener had no difficulty in passing since the opponents were vulnerable:

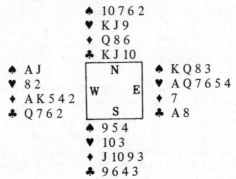

The defence slipped and did not extract the full penalty. Best defence brings in 1700, rather rare against the opponents' best suit at the one level.

A hand from the Spring Foursomes some ten years ago provoked a heated theoretical post-mortem:

♠ K 9 6   ♥ A K 8 6   ♦ K 10 6   ♣ Q J 4

At Game All, the bidding was:

1♥	Dble	Rdble	Pass
Pass	1♠	Pass	Pass
?			

The discussion centred around the merits of 1NT or 2NT, one faction arguing that 1NT had to be reserved for a minimum opening that had no more suitable rebid, the other argument being that opener should rebid normally as though partner had responded 1♠. Although game in no-trumps could be made, it was by no means certain, and the solution at the other table was a consultative double which collected 800.

3 When opener and responder have each had the opportunity of bidding twice they will have a good idea of their own fit and potential. It will usually make most sense to treat a double as consultative.

1♦	1♥	1♠	Pass
2♣	Pass	2♦	2♥
Dble			

What is the meaning of the final double? Opener has values in reserve, but has preferred the double to 2♠ or 3♦. It is not certain that the opponents have an eight-card fit. The double is consultative, and partner should remove it or stand it depending on whether his hand is weak or strong defensively within the context of his bidding.

These low level doubles entail a certain risk, and require fine partnership understanding.

Playing pairs, with neither side vulnerable, the bidding proceeds:

1♠	2♣	Dble (neg)	Pass
2♦	3♣	Pass	Pass
?			

If the Sputnik double promises a seven count and values in the red suits, what is the best bid on:

♠ A 10 8 3 2   ♥ K 6   ♦ A K 8 4   ♣ 9 8

This is a strong hand in defence and attack, and is worth another bid. 3♦ is the safe bid, but with an expert partner a consultative double is better. The layout could be:

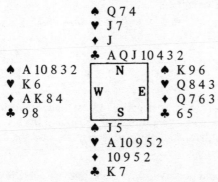

as it was in the London Duplicate Congress of 1980, and there is no defence to 3♣ or it might be:

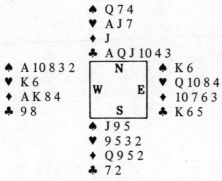

where 3♣ can be beaten by three tricks.

4 The last hand introduces the idea of doubling consultatively with the hand sitting under the opponent's trump holding. Is it better to double the opponents at the three level holding K-x-x under the trump suit, or with a doubleton and find partner with K-x-x? This, to some extent begs the question, because the doubler who holds two small trumps does not know that his

partner holds K-x-x, this is what he hopes for according to the bidding and the concept of total distribution.

In the 1980 Gold Cup the following hand was dealt at Love All:

♠ 6   ♥ A Q 9 7 5 4   ♦ A 7 4   ♣ 10 8 7

and the bidding procceeded:

1♠	Pass	2♥	2NT
Pass	3♣	?	

2NT shows the minors, and of course there is no guarantee that the opponents have a fit. The double brings in 300 with no game on.

From the 1980 Master Pairs:

♠ 9 7 6 4   ♥ 7   ♦ 10 3   ♣ A Q 8 7 5 2

and the bidding went:

1♣	Pass	1♦	Pass
1♥	Pass	2♣	2♦
Pass	Pass	?	

1♣ was strong, and 1♦ was negative. If 2♦ had been bid on the first round, it would have had a conventional meaning. If this hand doubles partner knows he must have something in trumps to leave the double. He has, he does, and +500 is a top score.

Perhaps the most common use of the consultative double is when 1NT has been doubled and rescued to two of a suit. Suppose:

1NT	Dble	2♦	Pass
Pass	Dble		

Even if the doubler has diamonds as good as K-J-x-x it is not logical for partner to pass with a singleton and discover later that declarer had Q-10-x-x-x. The double is consultative.

Several years ago in a Crockford's match a weak no-trump escaped a very heavy penalty because the defenders' methods were not adequately defined:

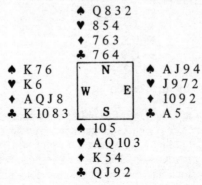

```
              ♠ Q 8 3 2
              ♥ 8 5 4
              ♦ 7 6 3
              ♣ 7 6 4
   ♠ K 7 6        N        ♠ A J 9 4
   ♥ K 6                   ♥ J 9 7 2
   ♦ A Q J 8  W       E    ♦ 10 9 2
   ♣ K 10 8 3      S       ♣ A 5
              ♠ 10 5
              ♥ A Q 10 3
              ♦ K 5 4
              ♣ Q J 9 2
```

South	West	North	East
–	–	–	Pass
1NT	Dble	2♥	Dble
2♠	Pass	Pass	Dble
Pass	2NT	Pass	3NT
All Pass			

2♥ was a transfer to spades, and the defenders' agreed methods were simply, 'double a transfer to show the suit, bid their suit for take-out'. In view of his spade holding, West thought the double of 2♠ must be for take-out. Against 2♠ doubled the defenders can draw all the trumps, and play diamonds, but cannot quite get the entries right to squeeze declarer for the seventh undertrick. The consultative double of 2♠ by West works wonders. 'Work-them-out-at-the-table' doubles go astray when the enemy does something strange.

5 Doubles of pre-emptive overcalls.

1♣   3♠   Dble

The double could show K-J-x-x in spades and not much else, but more frequently it will be made with three spades to an honour and scattered values outside. Opener will generally adopt the philosophy that 'if you are fixed, stay fixed', and will usually bend his endeavours to extracting whatever can be gained from 3♠ doubled. But the double is defined as consultative since opener may decide to have a try at 3NT with values in reserve.

1♠   4♥   Dble

The same principles apply. The double is no surprise to the player who bid 4♥, and the hand may not contain a trump trick. What is responder expected to do with:

♠ J 6   ♥ 10 7 3   ♦ A Q 9 4 2   ♣ K 7 4

Is he supposed to pass? With a good spade suit and a singleton heart opener may take a view and run to 4♠.

Chapter 16
Sputnik

The negative double of an opponent's overcall is widely used in tournament bridge. It is less common at rubber bridge, and even in tournament play there are highly qualified experts who choose not to employ it except in certain isolated sequences. The case against the negative or Sputnik double is that it abandons the penalty double when it is most needed. For it is when an opponent first ventures into the auction against the balance of high card points, and finds no fit, that a heavy penalty can be extracted from a deal which will only yield a part-score. There may also be an unseen cost: without the threat of an immediate penalty double opponents may take greater liberties with their overcalls, find more fits of their own, and generally make life difficult for the opening side.

The theoretical arguments for and against Sputnik are strong, and an aspiring partnership would be well advised to give each method an adequate trial period and judge by results.

The Sputnik double which gains almost universal approval from the experts is when one of the minors is overcalled by 1♠, now a double should show a hand which would have responded 1♥. Without this agreement a hand such as:

♠ 10 7 3   ♥ K J 9 7   ♦ K 7 6 2   ♣ Q 6

becomes unbiddable after: 1♣ - 1♠.

The only feature common to all varieties of Sputnik is that the double of an overcall is no longer for penalties. Instead it is used as an aid to constructive bidding. The double says nothing about the holding in the opponent's suit, in fact it often denies a secure stop in their suit. In most cases some length in at least one of the unbid suits is specified.

How strong is Sputnik?

There are two types of Sputnik, limited and high-powered. Limited Sputnik means that responder has a hand worth a response that has no satisfactory bid, and denies a game going hand. Opener bids on the assumption that his that his partner has a maximum of ten, eleven, or twelve points. High-powered Spunik implies that there is no maximum limit. The double is merely the first move on a good hand. The object of high-powered Sputnik is to allow responder to contest the auction by bidding a good suit at the two or three level with no outside values. Partner cannot misunderstand, since if responder had a good hand he would start by doubling.

The lower limit of the Sputnik double is largely a matter of common sense, and follows from the definition of 'a hand worth a response that has no satisfactory natural bid'.

♠ 8 6   ♥ 9 4   ♦ A 10 4 3   ♣ Q 9 8 6 3

After 1♥ - 1♠ this hand does not match up to the requirements for a response at the two level. But 1♠ passed out, or 2♠ passed out if fourth hand raises is unlikely to be a good score. Some partnerships re-open the bidding with a sound minimum opening bid, and with this understanding it is less necessary to bid on a hand such as this, but without this understanding, and it will be argued later that the method is unsound, the odds favour a negative double. Partner will bid 1NT with a spade stop, show a second suit, or, as a last resort, rebid his hearts. If partner cannot make whatever contract he bids it is highly probable that the opponents could have made 2♠ or more. With the same hand, if the bidding were: 1♠ - 2♥ the minors would have to be bid at the three level; the double is rather thin, and not to be recommended except at favourable vulnerability. Dependent on the tactical considerations of vulnerability, and the ranking of the suits, the lower level of Sputnik is seven points. That is what partner is entitled to expect.

The upper limit of Sputnik is more controversial. One way of playing limited Sputnik is to agree that responses at the two level will proceed as without the interference. Thus if the system requires eleven points for a response at the two level, the double denies these values. This seems tidy, but there are always awkward hands with eleven points or more which have no convenient bid:

♠ K J 4 3   ♥ A J 6 2   ♦ A 3 2   ♣ 9 6

after the bidding: 1♦ - 2♣, for example, and:

♠ 8 7 5 4   ♥ K 9 7 2   ♦ A K   ♣ K J 3

after the bidding: 1♦ - 1♠.

The most satisfactory arrangement is that responder's double shows 7-10 points. If he has more, then the onus is on him to catch up later.

High-powered Sputnik is one of the basically unsound methods which even experts are prepared to play provided it gains more than it loses. The cost of the privilege of being able to bid a good suit with very few high card values is that any good responding hand must start with a double regardless of its point count and distribution. If the defending side remains silent there will be no subsequent problems, the high-powered bidders will sort themselves out quite adequately. But after: 1♣ - 1♠ - Dble - 3♠, if 1♣ shows 11-19 and double shows 8-16 and any distribution in the red suits, any contract reached by the opening side could be loosely classified as random. Certainly no-one should pay them the compliment of sacrificing in 4♠ without very good reason. Against high-powered Sputnik the TNT raise is supreme. The jump in a new suit is another superb anti-Sputnik device: 1♣ - 1♠ - Dble - 3♦, the bid of 3♦ shows a good suit and a partial fit for partner.

♠ Q 3   ♥ J 8 7 4   ♦ A Q 10 6 5 3   ♣ 2

would be typical at any vulnerability. Partner can pass, correct to 3♠, raise or bid 4♠.

What level Sputnik?

When playing more than two or three boards against the same opponents it is always a good policy to find out what type of Sputnik they play. If they play negative doubles all the way to the five level, it is shrewd tactics to loosen up with pre-empts and weak jump overcalls. Conversely if an opponent asks what type of Sputnik you play, the answer is that it depends on the nature of the overcall. The optimum policy is probably: Sputnik against simple overcalls and strong jump overcalls, but penalty doubles of weak or intermediate jump overcalls. Doubles of pre-empts at the three level primarily for penalties. At the four level and higher the double may not necessarily contain a trump trick, but will be based on general values and is biased towards penalties.

When not to use Sputnik

You cannot double an opponent's overcall with values in his suit. Either pass or bid no-trumps.

Say the bidding proceeds: 1♠ - 2♦ and you hold:

♠ Q 9 4   ♥ A 2   ♦ Q 10 8 3   ♣ Q 10 4 2

What you bid on this hand depends on the vulnerability. If you are vulnerable against non-vulnerable, press for game with 2NT, Q-10-8-3 in their suit is as good as A-8-3. But if they are vulnerable, pass and hope that partner will re-open with a double which you will happily pass for penalties.

The fact that responder is often stuck for a bid with values in the opponent's suit gives rise to another common fallacy concerning Sputnik. That is re-opening with sound minimum values when an overcall is followed by two passes. The theory is that responder must have some values since the partner of the overcaller did not bid. The simple counter to that is not to respond to an overcall with a misfit and good values. The opening side will get into trouble. However, a word of caution is necessary. This ploy will only work against players whose ethics and mannerisms are impeccable. It is a quaint ruling of the governing body of bridge that if the bidding is: 1♣ - Pass - 1♦ - Pass a bid of 3NT by opener must be prefaced by the word 'Stop'. The reasons for the desirability or necessity of doing so are obscure. On the other hand if one intends to make an exclusive overcall such as 2♦ over 1♥, when one hopes that the next player will have a problem more often than not, one is not allowed to preface the bid by a polite request to the opponent not to bid quickly. The average player's ethics are average, why should they be anything else? The average responder thinks when he has a problem, and passes smoothly when he has no problem. The average opener has not considered what values are required to re-open the bidding, and will judge the situation when it occurs. The outcome is that the average pair does not get caught in the trap.

The problem of re-opening is no longer worrying if it is known that responder would have made a Sputnik double with as much as six or seven points, and will avoid trap passes if he can bid no-trumps. In a club system the problem recedes even further into insignificance. Opener is limited to fifteen or sixteen points, any further bidding is designed, by definition, to contest the part-score.

Opener's rebids

As a general rule opener should endeavour to make his natural rebid. If there is a choice between introducing a new suit economically and rebidding the original suit, the new suit is preferable.

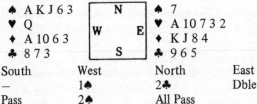

♠ A K J 6 3		♠ 7
♥ Q		♥ A 10 7 3 2
♦ A 10 6 3		♦ K J 8 4
♣ 8 7 3		♣ 9 6 5

South	West	North	East
–	1♠	2♣	Dble
Pass	2♠	All Pass	

The contract of 2♠ met with a suitably dismal fate.

No-trumps at minimum level should not imply extra values. After: 1♠ - 2♥ - Dble - Pass it is no more expensive to bid 2NT than to introduce a minor. 2NT may be just the bid that partner wants to hear if he has a good hand with no heart stop. If he does not like 2NT he can withdraw to three of a minor in the expectation of finding some support, and he has now shown a hand weaker than an immediate forcing bid of three of a minor.

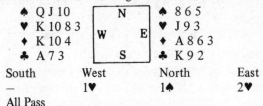

♠ Q J 10		♠ 8 6 5
♥ K 10 8 3		♥ J 9 3
♦ K 10 4		♦ A 8 6 3
♣ A 7 3		♣ K 9 2

South	West	North	East
–	1♥	1♠	2♥
All Pass			

Without Sputnik, 2♥ is more sensible than anything else. The contract of 2♥ failed when 1NT would have made. With Sputnik responder would double and opener would rebid 1NT.

The requirements for a Sputnik double

It is common practice for the Sputnik double to promise certain holdings in the unbid suits. If the opponents do not bid again this is unnecessary, but if they continue the barrage, opener will be very badly placed unless he knows he can rely on some measure of support for either of the unbid suits.

The correct way to approach the problem is to visualise the types of hand responder will hold where he cannot find a satisfactory bid, see what features they have in common, and then establish a basis for opener's rebids. If responder's hand does not contain the features he has 'promised!', he must be able to control the bidding.

The following is an analysis of Sputnik in conjunction with a strong artificial 1♣ opener and responses at the two level which promise eleven points. It may be necessary to introduce some modifications if the basic system is Acol.

1♦ - 1♥ - Dble
Responder declines to bid 1♠, 1NT, or 2♦. His hand will contain at least four clubs.

1♦ - 1♠ - Dble
Responder may have hearts or clubs and not have the values for a response at the two level. When responder has already passed, the requirements for a response at the two level are relaxed, a single good suit is bid more freely, and there is a strong inference that the double shows both unbid suits. If he has not passed there may be greater variation in his hand pattern. To enable opener to rebid accurately the double should promise a minimum of four hearts and three clubs.

♠ Q 4   ♥ K 10 3   ♦ A J 8 4 2   ♣ K 6 5

Opener should prefer a rebid of 2♥ to 1NT or 2♦. The worst that will happen is that it will be a 4-3 fit with the short trump hand being forced.

1♦ - 2♣ - Dble
Responder may have either major or both. Opener can bid a three-card major or rebid 2NT on a minimum hand. Because of the ranking of the suits opener will usually try to get the best of all possible worlds by rebidding his suit when in doubt.

♠ Q 4   ♥ K 10 3   ♦ A J 8 4 2   ♣ K 6 5

Rebid 2♦ and pass 2♥, but convert 2♠ to 2NT.

It will be dangerous for responder to double on a minimum hand without four cards in each major.

If responder produces a double after 1♥ - 2♣, 1♥ - 2♦, 1♠ - 2♣, 1♠ - 2♦ the sequence is similar in nature to 1♦ - 1♠ - Dble. The auction proceeds most smoothly if the double promises at least four cards in the unbid major and at least three in the unbid minor.

1♠ - 2♥ - Dble
If the double is constructive the hand will contain more than seven points. The emphasis is on the minors, but opener will freely rebid 2♠ or 2NT.

Responder may be as unbalanced as 6-4 in the minors with no more than 8-9 points.

The picture of Sputnik emerges as a negative double which shows the unbid suits. This is true, but there is one other type of hand which will double. A hand with trump support not good enough for an immediate raise. In Precision a doubleton honour; in Blue three to an honour. Thus for the sequence: 1♥ - 1♠ - Dble, responder may have:

♠ 10 6 5 2   ♥ K 9 3   ♦ 3   ♣ A Q 6 5 3

in the Blue Club, and:

♠ 10 6 5 2   ♥ K 3   ♦ 9 3   ♣ A Q 6 5 3

in the Precision Club.

The intention being to correct 2♦ to 2♥. The inference would be that responder does not have a minimum hand. Without the queen of clubs it would be more appropriate to raise immediately to 2♥.

It has already been suggested that opener should endeavour to make his natural rebid. Perhaps the easiest way to view the situation is this: If the bidding is: 1♦ - 1♠ - Dble - Pass imagine the bidding as: 1♦ - Pass - 1♥ - Pass and rebid accordingly; similarly imagine that: 1♥ - 2♣ - Dble was in fact: 1♥ - Pass - 1♠ - Pass, but be careful not to rebid 1NT.

Chapter 17
The Informative Double

The informative double must be nearly as old as the game itself. New ideas are unlikely to emerge. It is more a question of commenting on existing treatments.

There is a modern tendency to throw more and more strong hands into the catch-all of the take-out double. Strong one suiters, two suiters, flat hands of no-trump type containing a four-card major, three suiters with strength in the bid suit, all get bundled in. After an opening bid of 1♥ any of the following hands would find some players whose methods imposed a take-out double as the first move:

1	♠ 6	♥ Q 7 2	♦ A K Q 10 4 2	♣ K 8 3
2	♠ K 10 7 4 3	♥ Q 3	♦ A K J 9 8	♣ Q
3	♠ A Q 10 4 3	♥ 3	♦ A J 10 5 4 2	♣ 8
4	♠ A K 7 4 2	♥ A J 8	♦ 7 3	♣ K 10 4
5	♠ K Q 7 4	♥ A J 3 2	♦ K J 3 2	♣ 7

All of these hands are far removed from the original concept of the take-out double, which was regarded as the easiest and safest way of competing on moderate values with a good chance of a fit. It did not necessarily show a strong hand, but it did guarantee support for the unbid suits. Some players double with such a variety of unsuitable hands that they finish by maintaining that:

♠ K 8 3   ♥ 7   ♦ A J 9 5   ♣ K 9 8 4 3

is not a take-out double of 1♥. Their reason, apparently, is that the hand does not contain the magical number of four cards in the unbid major.

Why are the above hands unsuitable?

Hand 1
The hand is rather weak for a strong jump overcall to the three level, rather strong if the jump overcall is defined as intermediate. But either strong or intermediate, the jump overcall is vastly superior to a double which will almost certainly cause partner to misjudge the fit. Playing weak jump overcalls a simple overcall may conceal this type of hand.

Hand 2

Suppose this hand doubles and partner bids 3♣, either because he thinks his hand is worth it, or because the third hand bids 2♥. Now does a bid of 3♦ show this hand or a hand similar to Hand 1? The hand is better expressed by a simple overcall of 1♠. If third hand bids 2♥ which is followed by two passes, the hand is worth a bid of 3♦. It does not pay to be too reticent when the opponents have a fit and limited values.

Hand 3

Although the point count is low, the hand has tremendous potential if there is a fit. Partner needs only four to the king in one of the two suits to give a play for game. When this hand occurred the bidding, with both sides vulnerable, was:

1♥	Dble	4♥	Pass
Pass	?		

What would you bid? The hand passed and struck on the unfortunate lead of the ace of spades, followed by a small one when partner played the nine.

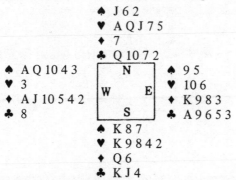

```
              ♠ J 6 2
              ♥ A Q J 7 5
              ♦ 7
              ♣ Q 10 7 2
♠ A Q 10 4 3      N       ♠ 9 5
♥ 3                       ♥ 10 6
♦ A J 10 5 4 2  W   E     ♦ K 9 8 3
♣ 8               S       ♣ A 9 6 5 3
              ♠ K 8 7
              ♥ K 9 8 4 2
              ♦ Q 6
              ♣ K J 4
```

So 4♥ was made with 6♦ an easy make the other way, and on a double dummy defence 2♥ can be beaten.

Two suited hands merit special treatment, and are seldom developed satisfactorily after a take-out double.

Hand 4

Partner will not bid a three-card spade suit in response to a double, nor in response to 1NT. If a 5-3 spade fit can be located, it may play well, but there may be the same number of tricks available in no-trumps. A simple overcall of 1♠ leaves so much in reserve that the player may feel obliged to bid again in a non-fit sequence. 1NT is the bid which best describes the hand.

Hand 5

The same problem again. If you double, partner bids clubs, and you correct to diamonds, does this show Hand 1, Hand 2, or Hand 5. An overcall of 1♠ comes to no harm on this type of hand.

Let us admit that in some quarters it is considered old-fashioned to guarantee three cards in each unbid suit for a take-out double. Nevertheless the advantage is that partner can immediately judge the fit, and bid it to its full extent. That is the theme of this outline of competitive bidding. Find your fit and bid it. Playing 'any-shape' doubles, what tends to happen is that the responder adopts the principle of leeway, naming his best suit at minimum level on any hand ranging from a Yarborough to a game force. The hand that doubled is obliged to bid again on the same values. This method is basically unsound, but is seldom caught out. The reason is that a redouble by the third hand relieves the doubler of the necessity to rebid. The crazy system works provided the opening side co-operates. But if third hand redoubles on six hearts to the jack and a bust, the opponents are likely to play in 1♠ making four overtricks, or if the third hand passes with values instead of making an ingenuous redouble, the opponents are in danger of walking into an unnecessary penalty. The hand below turned out very favourably for North-South.

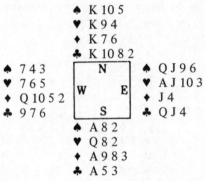

```
                    ♠ K 10 5
                    ♥ K 9 4
                    ♦ K 7 6
                    ♣ K 10 8 2
    ♠ 7 4 3          N          ♠ Q J 9 6
    ♥ 7 6 5                     ♥ A J 10 3
    ♦ Q 10 5 2   W     E        ♦ J 4
    ♣ 9 7 6          S          ♣ Q J 4
                    ♠ A 8 2
                    ♥ Q 8 2
                    ♦ A 9 8 3
                    ♣ A 5 3
```

With both sides vulnerable, North opened the bidding with 1♦ (strong club). East doubled, and South decided that there was no hurry to bid 3NT, it would be more amusing to see how far the opponents could get first, so he passed. West could not see anything to choose between his major suits, he bid 1NT, which came round to South, who was still in no hurry. He doubled. West did not like the prospect of 1NT doubled, and redoubled. East couldn't see anywhere to go, so she didn't go anywhere. This bizarre contract went for 1600. Since 3NT went two down in the other room the net loss was 1800.

Third hand bids

'A change of suit is not forcing since the hand is limited by the failure to redouble' Reese. After: 1♣ - Dble, since 1♥ or 1♠ is not forcing it will presumably show a five-card suit. This abandons hope of finding a 4-4 major fit unless third hand is strong enough to redouble. Even then if fourth hand can make a TNT raise, the 4-4 fit may still be lost. It suggests little faith in one's constructive bidding to abandon it as soon as some jester enters the auction with a light-hearted double. In fact if the opponents are going to create a bipartite system of bidding, half of which is to be put to use after a take-out double, then there may well be advantage to be gained from the occasional joke double just for the pleasure of listening to their plan B.

There may be some merit in some carefully worked out modifications to constructive bidding after a take-out double, but by far the simplest solution is to ignore the double. After: 1♦ - Dble, there is no better bid than a forcing response of 1♥ on any of the following hands:

♠ 3 2　♥ A Q 6 5　♦ Q 4 3　♣ J 5 4 2

♠ 3　♥ A Q 8 6 5　♦ Q 4 3　♣ Q 8 5 4

♠ 3　♥ A K 7 5 4 2　♦ K 4 3　♣ Q 5 4

The argument that the third hand is strong enough to redouble since the opponents will not go far is only valid against weak opponents. TNT raises are designed to find the chinks in the armour of faulty methods.

One expects some deference to high cards, and holding:

♠ 3　♥ A K 7 5 4 2　♦ K 4 3　♣ Q 5 4

there is no reason to anticipate:

1♦	Dble	Rdble	2♠
Pass	3♠ or 4♠	?	

but it could be a cautionary experience. The redouble asks partner to pass, he has done so, and responder's wish has been granted.

The fallacy of non-forcing responses after a double is pursued to its logical conclusion by some players who would bid 2♣ after: 1♠ - Dble, on:

♠ 6　♥ Q 8 7 2　♦ J 4 3　♣ K 10 7 4 3

Their argument that 1♠ doubled might be passed for penalties has all the attraction of taking an umbrella into an earthquake zone in case it rains.

If it is accepted that a response over the double is forcing, there is a good case to be made for a jump response to be non-forcing, showing a suit and a partial fit. The bid should show some 6-10 points. Non-vulnerable the bid acts as a limit bid in two suits, and may be stretched. Vulnerable the player should expect to make his contract. After: 1♦ - Dble

♠ 3　♥ A Q 8 6 5 4　♦ Q 4 3　♣ 10 5 4

is an ideal bid of 2♥ vulnerable. Non-vulnerable the hand should still bid 2♥, but 2♥ could also be bid on a hand which is much weaker.

♠ 9 5 4　♥ Q J 9 6 2　♦ K 10 3　♣ 8 4

expects to make eight tricks in one of the red suits or show a profit in the attempt.

Redouble

Redouble denies a fit with partner, and lays claim to the majority of the points. It asks for partner's co-operation in extracting a penalty from the opponents.

♠ 7 3   ♥ A J 10 3   ♦ K 9 2   ♣ K 8 7 5

is a typical redouble after: 1♠ - Dble. Partner will double 2♦ if he can. Preserve the same high cards, but change the suits to:

♠ A J 10 3   ♥ K 9 2   ♦ K 8 7 5   ♣ 7 3

After the bidding: 1♣ - Dble, this hand illustrates the weakness of accepted methods. There are two possible lines of approach, either bid constructively in search of a possible game, or try to penalise the opponents. The constructive approach is to bid 1♠ forcing. The best way to get a penalty is to pass, possibly forcing the next hand to bid when it does not want to, and increase the chances of getting a double at the two level. It is easy to see that redouble achieves neither of these objectives.

Since a redouble asks partner to pass or double the opponents, if he does neither, and bids in front of the redouble, he has a weak distributional hand.

1♥	Dble	Rdble	Pass
2♦ or 2♥			

This bidding shows a sub-minimum hand. If the hand were a full strength opening bid, it should pass and bid on the next round. The same distinction should be drawn between:

Pass	Pass	1♠	1NT
Dble	2♣	2♥	

and

Pass	Pass	1♠	1NT
Dble	2♣	Pass	Pass
Dble	Pass	2♥	

The second sequence shows a sound opening bid unsuitable in defence of 2♣.

There is, of course, one other way of bidding in front of partner:

1♥	Dble	Rdble	Pass
3♣			

Vulnerability is a consideration here. Trying to screw 300 out of 1♠ doubled is a waste of time if the opening side can make 630. In Acol 3♣ would be defined as game forcing; in a club system, opener's hand would be clearly expressed.

Chapter 18
Responding to a
Take-Out Double

Third hand passes

Since a response at minimum level will have to be made on a Yarborough, it is inappropriate to make the same bid on a hand which contains useful values. A jump to two of a major should show the values for a sound raise to the two level of partner's suit. Ideally the hand would hold five trumps, but after: 1♥ - Dble - Pass - ?, 2♠ is the only bid worth considering on:

♠ K Q 7 6   ♥ 9 5 4   ♦ K 3   ♣ 10 5 4 2

To bid only 1♠ on a hand such as this would put too much pressure on partner, and make it easy for opener to bid again. This jump to two of a major is a limit bid and a hand as strong as:

♠ K Q 10 6   ♥ 9 5 4   ♦ K 3   ♣ Q J 8 2

must find an alternative bid.

The jump to three of a minor must of necessity carry a wider range of hands. The bid is not forcing, but must nevertheless show good values since partner may have taken a chance on a minimum hand with a poor minor suit holding, whereas he would always be prepared for the unbid major.

A triple jump to three of a major is an inelegant bid and should be reserved for a long suit which has little interest in game.

Many players adopt an inferior strategy after a simple response to a take-out double:

1♦	Dble	Pass	1♠
2♦	2♠		

Often the bid of 2♠ is made on a minimum hand with spade support. The fallacy of this method would be demonstrated more frequently if third hand adopted the policy of trap passing on a hand which would normally redouble, 2♠ would be massacred if 1♠ had been bid on a three-card suit and a Yarborough. Superior technique is to expect responder to bid again if he has six or seven points, and in that case 2♠ would be interpreted as a sound competitive raise or a mild game try. If opener passes on the second round the same danger exists that the hand that doubled may be raising a non-existent suit, therefore a raise should show at least sound competitive values. When the doubler holds a hand which is worth a genuine game try he will cue-bid the opponent's suit, which will be understood to show primary support for partner's suit.

1♦	Dble	Pass	1♠
Pass	2♦		

the bid of 2♦ shows a strong raise to 2♠ which is interested in game if partner has a maximum one bid. It will also be the first move on a stronger hand worth a raise to 3♠ or 4♠, as a precaution against partner holding a worthless hand. Responder should avoid a minimum rebid of his suit if he has a working five or six count, and it follows that if the doubler proceeds in spite of a sign off he is interested in game opposite three or four points in the right places.

Without this understanding about the cue-bid

♠ A Q 9 3   ♥ 4   ♦ A Q J 4 2   ♣ K Q 9

would double 1♥ and face a problem over the response of 1♠. A pessimist, aware of the dangers, might settle for 3♠; an optimist would bid game on the grounds that partner will pass 3♠ with:

♠ K J 8 2   ♥ 8 7 5 2   ♦ 10 9 3   ♣ 8 3

Using the cue-bid these hands would bid:

1♥	Dble	Pass	1♠
Pass	2♥	Pass	2♠
Pass	3♦	Pass	4♠
All Pass			

When responder has been obliged to bid on a useless hand the final contract may not make, but there may be a considerable saving in staying one level lower and avoiding a costly double.

In response to the take-out double the cue-bid of the opponent's suit used to be regarded as a game force. The modern approach is to treat it as forcing to 2NT or suit agreement, for this loses nothing on genuine game going hands and gains on the hands which wish to invite game but are not strong enough to insist on it. A hand such as:

♠ A 10 8 6 3   ♥ J 3   ♦ K 6 3   ♣ Q J 2

is a value raise to 3♠ if partner doubles 1♦. The technique is to start with 2♦, if partner bids 2♥, 2♠ will be forcing, and it is understood that he will bid 4♠ if he can. If he only bids 3♠ this will be passed.

After partner has doubled 1♦, there is no convenient bid on:

♠ Q 2   ♥ K J 3 2   ♦ A 10 8 5   ♣ 10 6 4

The best choice is 2♦, with the intention of raising 2♥ to 3♥, which of course denies the ability to bid game. Over the more likely rebid of 2♠, 2NT will suggest a four-card heart suit, since a hand worth 2NT that has no interest in the majors would have bid it on the first round.

Two other bids remain, 1NT and the penalty pass. 1NT in response to a double of 1♣ is clearly a stronger bid than if the suit doubled is spades, over spade there may be nowhere else to go unless it is agreed that 2♣ might be bid as a total denial. Even in response to the double of 1♣ it should not be automatically assumed that 1NT shows 8-10 points. Particularly at pairs scoring 1NT is a tactical bid which may be an effort to exclude the majors. In both the sequences: 1♣ - Dble - 1NT and 1♣ - Dble - Pass - 1NT, 1NT may be short of the theoretical number of points required. At pairs scoring with neither side vulnerable, if there is a choice of playing 1NT or allowing the opponents to do so, there is no doubt which is preferable.

The penalty pass of a take-out double is used too frequently in non-expert circles. For a penalty pass to show a profit against non-vulnerable opponents, it is necessary to make a contract at the two level in the opponent's suit. Not vulnerable against vulnerable opponents the penalty pass is more likely to succeed, one off beats any part-score, and two off is excellent compensation for the loss of a game.

After a redouble
In the mists of antiquity it was thought that a pass over a redouble should be for penalties, showing a suit such as Q-J-10-9-x-x and nothing much outside. Many advocates of this method are still waiting for an appropriate hand to be dealt. In fact a hand such as this did occur some sixteen years ago in the Ladies Team Olympiad of 1964:

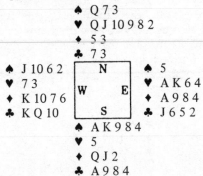

```
                    ♠ Q 7 3
                    ♥ Q J 10 9 8 2
                    ♦ 5 3
                    ♣ 7 3
    ♠ J 10 6 2          N           ♠ 5
    ♥ 7 3                            ♥ A K 6 4
    ♦ K 10 7 6      W       E        ♦ A 9 8 4
    ♣ K Q 10            S            ♣ J 6 5 2
                    ♠ A K 9 8 4
                    ♥ 5
                    ♦ Q J 2
                    ♣ A 9 8 4
```

East opened 1♥ which was doubled, redoubled and passed out. South led the ace of spades. Though it is standard practice to lead a trump, as it happens only a club lead can defeat the contract.

It must be extremely depressing to carry around in your head for a decade or so a bidding sequence which never occurs, and then when it finally does come up you find yourself presenting the opponents with the easiest game contract of all on a hand ideal for your system.

Pass over the redouble should mean a flat hand that has nothing to say, partner can make his own arrangements, if he wants help he can bid something and redouble.

A minimum bid does not guarantee values. Holding:

       ♠ 9 2   ♥ Q 9 6 5   ♦ 10 7 5 4   ♣ 8 7 3

if 1♦ is doubled and redoubled, a pass might result in partner playing the hand in 1♠ doubled. The bid of 1♥ is no more than an opinion that this might be the safest refuge.

Whenever possible fourth hand should not hesitate to jump the bidding after the redouble. A TNT raise on the assumption that partner has three-card support is the best way to bid one's hand and make life difficult for the opponents, presenting problems in particular to hands which have redoubled on unsuitable holdings.

In theory fourth hand cannot hold much in the way of high cards. Thirteen points for the opener, thirteen for the doubler and eleven for the redouble, leaves three points. In practice players shade their bids and fourth hand sometimes has quite strong values. If, after 1♦ has been redoubled, it is correct to bid 2♠ on:

♠ K J 9 6 3　♥ 8 2　♦ 10 4 3　♣ Q 10 6

It cannot be correct to bid 2♠ on:

♠ K J 9 6 3　♥ 8　♦ 10 4 3　♣ A J 6 2

A variety of manoeuvres commend themselves. A leap to three or four spades is a possibility, hoping that it is not partner who has borrowed some of these high cards for his bid. A calculated underbid of 1♠ may turn out well. But often the best policy is to believe the three opponents that you have not got anything, and bid accordingly. Exposing psyches is a waste of time, it is far better to pass and try to give the impression of being in trouble or committing an indiscretion later in the auction.

There is seldom any hurry to bid on a good hand over a redouble, as the deal below shows:

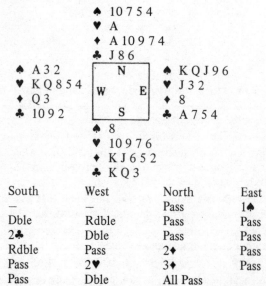

| ♠ 10 7 5 4 |
| ♥ A |
| ♦ A 10 9 7 4 |
| ♣ J 8 6 |

South	West	North	East
—	—	Pass	1♠
Dble	Rdble	Pass	Pass
2♣	Dble	Pass	Pass
Rdble	Pass	2♦	Pass
Pass	2♥	3♦	Pass
Pass	Dble	All Pass	

The auction developed very nicely for North. He did not have to reveal himself too soon, and was not even obliged to go to the four level.

Third hand bids a new suit

After a sequence such as: 1♣ - Dble 1♠ TNT raises are played in the unbid suits. 1NT shows a guard in the danger suit, clubs, for partner has promised something in spades.

One of a major by third hand on a non-existent suit is so common that it is referred to as a baby psyche. It should not succeed against moderately competent players. If the opponents are playing forcing responses over a double there is no hurry to expose the psyche, it may rebound if fourth hand passes. But if the response is non-forcing, and fourth hand holds spades, he may decide to expose the psyche immediately. Double would show four spades and at least the values for a sound raise of 1♠ to 2♠, partner should raise 'your' suit accordingly. To bid 2♠ shows a five-card suit, and is a limit bid, a hand stronger than a limit raise to 2♠ should cue-bid 2♣ and then bid 2♠ which is forcing to suit agreement.

Third hand raises

After: 1♦ - Dble - 2♦ fourth hand should make any obvious value bid. Three of a major should be construed as invitational, for there is no point in pre-empting against opponents who have found a fit and made a limit bid. 3♦ and 4♦ asks partner to choose a major at the appropriate level. Double is responsive, partner is not entitled to expect any more than the values to contest at the two level. Players frequently abuse this responsive double, passing the buck to partner when they should make the decision themselves. Holding:

♠ K 10 6 5   ♥ J 10 3   ♦ K 8 6 2   ♣ J 3

it is very chicken hearted not to weigh in with 2♠. To double responsively is foolish, partner will bid a four-card heart suit, be forced on a diamond lead, and lose control. Perhaps there is more excuse for a double on this type of hand if partner is in the habit of making take-out doubles on a wide variety of hand patterns; but that is an argument against any-shape doubles rather than a solution to this hand. Any action on this hand risks a 4-3 major fit, the 4-3 heart fit is a potential disaster, the 4-3 spade fit a potential top.

Convenient hands for the responsive double are to be found chiefly in text books, and even then the double is usually illustrated by a hand which is worth 3♦. If you intend to raise either of partner's majors to the three level, regardless of which he bids, then you have a 3♦ bid. At the table one either holds some collection of small cards, or some awkward hand such as:

♠ K 8 3   ♥ 9 6   ♦ K 10 4 2   ♣ A 10 4 3

where any action may prove wrong. This is where it is necessary to have a good partnership understanding on the responsive double. It is just this sort of hand which must double, because nothing else makes sense. If partner bids

2♥, which is almost inevitable, bid 2♠, and he should be able to work out that you will be quite happy if he corrects to 3♣. Why else should you double and correct 2♥ to 2♠? If 2♠ appears too dangerous try 2NT over 2♥, it won't necessarily be a better contract, but there is the same inference that partner can correct to 3♣.

If after the responsive double, opener continues with 3♦, partner is absolved from the necessity of finding another bid, driving the opponents to the three level may have been one of the objectives of the responsive double. However, he may decide that if you have the values to compete at the two level, then he wishes to compete at the three level, and he will double again or bid a major.

To what level should a double be responsive? Most players would go at least as far as 3♦. If the double of 3♠ is to be responsive, there must be a good case for including four of a minor, players who raise 1♦ to 4♦ usually have a long string of diamonds and not much else, and the TNT is likely to be high enough to make four of a major playable in defence. The double can help in choosing the right major. Wherever the line is drawn it is an arbitrary decision, but the argument to include 3♥ but not 3♠ is attractive, and consistent with what has been suggested for competitive doubles. There is no great advantage in doubling 3♠ for the minors, but after a raise to 3♥ there is still a contract at the three level, one which they are probably trying to shut out. The responsive double of 3♥ should convey a clear message about the spade suit. A contract at the three level with a trump holding of K-x-x opposite J-x-x-x is unlikely to play well, particularly since it is common practice for opener to bid 1♥ with four cards in both majors. The number of spades is not a sufficient guide. The quality of the suit, and which hand will be forced, are equally important considerations. Responder must not be afraid to bid a suit headed by two honours just because it is only a four-card suit, it is dummy which will accept the force. Therefore it should be assumed that the double shows a weak four-card spade suit or three to an honour, and tolerance for the minors.

Chapter 19
Responding to an Overcall

In comparison to the amount of bidding theory which has evolved around the opening bid and response, the response to an overcall is almost entirely neglected. Current theory could be summarised as:

1   A change of suit is non-forcing and does not imply support for partner's suit.

2   A jump in a new suit is a one round force.

3   The cue-bid in the opponent's suit is a general purpose force, asking partner for another suit or extra strength.

That is it, as far as theory is concerned. In practice nine times out of ten partner rebids his own suit at minimum level confirming a single suited hand of limited ambition, (precisely what is expected of a simple overcall) and responder is left in the same position as he was on the previous round.

Simple overcalls can be classified into three types, which, for want of a better term, will be called exclusive, semi-exclusive, and non-exclusive. There are four cases of each type.

Exclusive:	1	1♣	1♠
	2	1♦	2♣
	3	1♥	2♦
	4	1♠	2♥
Semi-exclusive:	1	1♣	1♥
	2	1♦	1♠
	3	1♥	2♣
	4	1♠	2♦
Non-exclusive:	1	1♣	1♦
	2	1♦	1♥
	3	1♥	1♠
	4	1♠	2♣

An exclusive overcall is so called because it excludes the remaining two suits from the auction at minimum level. A semi-exclusive overcall excludes one suit only.

Any overcall may serve its purpose if it indicates a damaging lead. To that end many players overcall on hands with a good suit and little else. Such overcalls are part of the game, but from the point of view of constructive bidding they are irrelevant. An exclusive overcall does most damage to the opponents' bidding; that is the overcall that one should strive to produce. Holding a hand such as:

♠ K J 9 7 3   ♥ J 2   ♦ 10 8 7   ♣ A 3 2

there is more merit in butting in with 1♠ if the opening bid was 1♣ than if it was 1♥. Because of its greater nuisance value an exclusive overcall may contain less values than a non-exclusive overcall. The common use of the Sputnik double which was designed primarily to combat exclusive overcalls testifies to their effectiveness.

There is another side to exclusive overcalls. Second hand bends over backwards to produce one, it transpires later that third hand was merely making up the number, and it is partner who is excluded. In a system of constructive bidding this must be taken into account.

Exclusive overcalls

The following is the scheme of responses proposed for the sequence:

1♣   1♠   Pass   ?

Any raise in spades — pre-emptive.

3♣ — the game invitation in spades, partner may pass the decision back with a bid of 3♦ or 3♥. He may sign off in 3♠, bid 4♠, or a precautionary 3NT.

4♣ — a high card raise to game in spades. It will be more necessary to distinguish between 4♣ and 4♠ when third hand has produced a Sputnik double or a raise in clubs.

3♦, 3♥ — Here there is a departure from accepted practice. This bid shows a six-card suit (possibly a good five-card suit) and a partial fit for partner's suit. A partial fit would be a doubleton honour or three small. The strength of the hand is dependent on the vulnerability and the strength of the overcall. One expects to make the contract. Partner is invited to pass or correct to his own suit, on occasions he may be in a position to raise the suit.

2♣ — In the first instance partner should treat this bid in the same way as a competitive double. Normal practice is to define this cue-bid as a sound raise to 2♠. The idea is ill-conceived. If partner takes the trouble to make an exclusive overcall cutting out the red suits, it is obtuse of responder to make a bid which allows the red suits back in to the auction when he has no interest in them. A sound raise to 2♠ should bid 2♠. There is no law against having some high cards to substantiate one's bidding. It is sometimes quite a good idea. If the bid is used as a sort of competitive double, responder, ideally, will be 5-5 in the reds, the overcaller will bid a three-card red suit and that will be the contract. Responder will also use the bid on a hand such as:

♠ J 3   ♥ A Q 9 3 2   ♦ K 6 3   ♣ J 10 7
or
♠ J 3   ♥ K 6 3   ♦ A Q 9 3 2   ♣ J 10 7

On the first hand 2♦ will be corrected to 2♥ which partner is free to correct to 2♠. On the second hand 2♦ will be passed, and 2♥ will be corrected by responder to 2♠.

The cue-bid of the opponent's suit can also be employed on a stronger hand:

1♣	1♠	Pass	2♣
Pass	2♦	Pass	2♠

The inference is that responder is not interested in the red suits, therefore he has the values for a raise to 3♠, but only three trumps, a hand such as:

> ♠ A 10 3   ♥ Q 3   ♦ K 10 3 2   ♣ A 9 8 5

With a fourth trump:

> ♠ A 10 3 2   ♥ Q 3   ♦ K 10 3   ♣ A 9 8 5

responder is more certain that the TNT is higher, and would have bid 3♣ on the first round.

1♣	1♠	Pass	2♣
Pass	2♥	Pass	2♠

The inference is no longer valid. Responder may have been angling for 2♦ and is now settling for 2♠. He has:

> ♠ J 3   ♥ K 6 3   ♦ A Q 9 3 2   ♣ J 10 7

or less.

Now consider:

1♣	1♠	Pass	2♣
Pass	2♥	Pass	3♦

or

1♣	1♠	Pass	2♣
Pass	2♦	Pass	3♥

Facing a simple overcall containing five or six spades and three or four in the wrong red suit, it is unrealistic to define responder's second bid as forcing. It shows a very strong hand similar to a strong jump overcall and is highly encouraging.

1♣	1♠	Pass	2♣
Pass	2♦ or 2♥	Pass	3♠

Responder has a good opening bid with three-card spade support. 3♠ can be passed, but partner is invited to attempt 3NT or 4♠.

1♣	1♠	Pass	2♣
Pass	3♦		

The overcaller has a sound bid and has a second suit. If responder has a five-card heart suit and a moderate hand he will pass 3♦ or correct to 3♠. A correction to 3♠ is not invitational, responder knows almost exactly what to expect from his partner, and 3♠ denies the ability to bid game.

It follows from this use of the cue-bid in the opponent's suit that a change of suit opposite an exclusive overcall denies a fit with partner. For the bidding: 1♣ - 1♠ - Pass 2♥, responder has something like:

♠ 3   ♥ K J 9 8 3 2   ♦ Q 6 3   ♣ J 7 2

or

♠ 3   ♥ K Q 9 7 4 2   ♦ A 3   ♣ Q 6 5 2

since

♠ Q 3   ♥ K J 9 8 3 2   ♦ 6 3   ♣ J 7 2

or

♠ Q 3   ♥ K 9 7 4 3 2   ♦ A 3   ♣ Q 6 5

would bid 2♣ and not 2♥.

There remains one other alternative after: 1♣ - 1♠ - Pass and that is 1NT, which will be bid with a partial fit or no fit with partner. With no fit the hand will be stronger.

♠ 3   ♥ K J 6 3   ♦ Q J 8 2   ♣ A 10 8 3

or

♠ K 3   ♥ Q J 2   ♦ Q 10 7 6   ♣ J 10 8 2

would be typical. Partner is not expected to retreat to two of his suit, but is free to introduce a second suit if he sees fit to do so. It is worth noting that if the suits are changed round on the first hand to:

♠ K J 6 3   ♥ Q J 8 2   ♦ A 10 8 3   ♣ 3

after: 1♦ - 2♣ - Pass, 2♦ asking for a three-card major is likely to find the best scoring contract in a pairs contest.

Before leaving exclusive overcalls, it is necessary to take a view on a sequence such as: 1♠ - 2♥ - Pass - 3♣ or 3♦. According to the schedule above 2♠ would invite partner to show a three-card minor, therefore 3♣ or 3♦ is correction of contract and denies a fit with partner. It should be added however, that correcting two of a major to three of a minor is a dubious manoeuvre likely to gain neither points nor partner's approval.

Semi-exclusive overcalls

1♥   2♣   Pass   ?

2♦ — A suit worth showing, neither denies or affirms a fit with partner. In practice partner will usually pass unless he hates it, since he must increase the level to rebid his own suit.

2♥ — It costs nothing to have the understanding that partner will show a fragment in the excluded suit, in this case spades. But since there is only one excluded suit 2♥ will usually be a good raise to 3♣, and if that is the case overcaller may venture 2NT with no spade support.

2♠ — In view of the use of 2♥ this is to play and denies a fit in clubs.

2NT — It is bad technique to bid this from dislike of clubs. The successful way to treat the bid is competitive showing at least a partial fit with a partner. He is free to run to clubs if he does not think his suit is running. Note that 1NT and 2NT are different species.

Non-exclusive overcalls

1♦	1♥	Pass	?

1♠, 2♣ — A suit. In terms of a heart fit the bid is neutral.

2♦ — A hand worth 2♥ but strong in defence. Partner should press to 3♥ in competition only if he expects to make it. If he is top weight for his overcall he may rebid 3♥ or show another suit. His normal course of action will be to bid 2♥. 2♠ by responder should now be treated as a one round force. Two of the unbid major after a cue-bid will also be a one round force in other variations. For example:

1♣	1♦	Pass	2♣
Pass	2♦	Pass	2♥ or 2♠

3♦ — The game try in hearts.

2♠, 3♣ — Good suit, non-forcing, at least a partial fit in partner's suit.

The scheme of bidding outlined above, in common with any other method, works most efficiently when partner's bid describes hands of a narrow range of points and playing strength. If partner's overcall may show 6-16 points the subsequent bidding will be largely random from the point of view of the defence. The simple overcall must be limited by the alternative bids available, namely the double, the 1NT overcall, and the jump overcall. The simple overcall should not, in principle, contain more than fourteen points. A double or an off-beat 1NT is generally preferable on a fifteen count. Responder will assume that the lower limit is an eight count. If overcaller has less than eight points that is his affair. He may suspect that his side's bidding is sacrificial, and he can but hope that he has found something worthwhile against which to sacrifice.

The meaning assigned to jump overcalls has its effects on the simple overcall. The Acol style jump overcall is rather similar to the Acol Two bid which Reese finds 'not always impressive'. Though 'it's presence is reassuring', 'it may prove both ponderous and vulnerable'. The two bids have several features in common. Their existence is justified chiefly by the negative inferences of their non-appearance. On the infrequent occasions when they lumber into motion responder's problem is usually confined to whether he wishes his partner to play a game or a part-score. The bids themselves create no problems for the opponents who know they are missing nothing, consequently any bid they make is by necessity defensive.

The weak jump overcall is a destructive manoeuvre paid for at the cost of accuracy in constructive bidding. If the jump overcall is weak, hands which might be described constructively by a jump overcall must find some other means of expression, either the simple overcall or the double must take the strain. The weak jump can be a great annoyance, and is often effective against timid players, but it is easily doubled for penalties, and is best reserved for use against a strong club system where constructive bidding is unusual.

The advantage of the intermediate style jump overcall is that it occurs far more frequently than the strong variety, and the opponents cannot relax in the knowledge that they are not missing anything. Neither can they double too freely, one high card and a ruffing value in dummy may be all that is needed to make the contract.

The apparent disadvantage of the intermediate jump overcall is that if a simple overcall shows 8-14 points, and a jump overcall shows 10-14 points or the equivalent playing strength, there is a duplication of bids. A knowledge of TNT theory refutes this argument. Points in a competitive auction are no more important than trump length. The jump overcall shows six, possibly seven trumps. The simple overcall promises only five, and may be made on a good four-card suit at the one level. Holding:

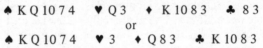

♠ A Q 10 4   ♥ 7 2   ♦ A 9 4   ♣ K 10 7 3

is there a better bid than 1♠ over 1♣?

The idea than an overcall is unsuitable on a hand which contains values in the suit bid on the right is an archaic gentlemanly agreement designed to ensure that the opponents never go wrong. Admittedly this is part of traditional bidding theory, but such beliefs cannot expect to go unchallenged in the modern game, merely because they are traditional. Which of the following two hands is more suitable for an overcall of 1♠ over 1♣?

♠ K Q 10 7 4   ♥ Q 3   ♦ K 10 8 3   ♣ 8 3

or

♠ K Q 10 7 4   ♥ 3   ♦ Q 8 3   ♣ K 10 8 3

In the first case the high cards in clubs are likely to lie favourably for the opening side, and a possible over-ruffing situation also favours the opening side. On the second hand both the position of the honour cards and the potential over-ruff favours the defending side. The second hand is far stronger offensively and defensively, and it is on this hand that a defender has most interest in joining battle. The belief that an overcall has little potential in defence dates from the age of chivalry when it was considered good form to charge the enemy with an empty musket.

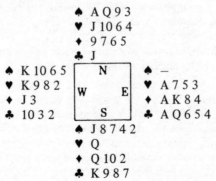

This hand was dealt in the second session of the pairs tournament of the London Duplicate Congress of 1980. With East-West vulnerable, the bidding was:

South	West	North	East
–	–	–	1♣
1♠	1NT	3♠	3NT
All Pass			

A small spade to the jack was ducked by declarer. He covered the spade continuation, and won the diamond switch in dummy, having discarded a small heart and a small diamond from the dummy. A small club from the dummy seemed the best line, and thereafter declarer made no more than his five top tricks. Twenty years ago, South would have held A-Q-J-x-x in spades and a small doubleton club and 3NT would have made in comfort.

Chapter 20
Two Suiters

A take-out double on a two suiter is bad for three reasons. First partner cannot judge the fit if he finds no support at all for his best suit. Secondly, the subsequent auction is not always clear. Suppose the bidding is:

1♦	Dble	2♦	3♣
3♦	3♥		

does 3♥ guarantee 5-5 in the majors, in which case partner should bid 3♠ or 4♠ with a three-card spade holding? Or is 3♥ an effort to outrank the opponents, and if partner does not like it he can return to 4♣? Thirdly, the difference in the number of tricks which a two suiter yields with a fit and a misfit is quite astonishing to anyone unfamiliar with TNT theory.

Consider:

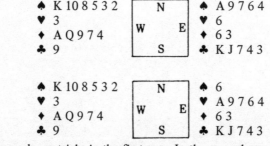

and

Ten or eleven tricks in the first case. In the second case any contract above the two level risks being catastrophic. There is no guarantee that the hand will produce more than five or six tricks. If the spade-diamond two suiter doubles 1♣ the hand produces five tricks more if responder has the right major. Admittedly the enemy might bid differently, but a system of bidding which requires their assistance is not a good system.

For the last reason alone two suiters merit special treatment. With more than five losers, make a simple overcall, and guess whether or not to show the second suit on the next round. With four or five losers use a conventional overcall. Quantum has the advantage over Ghestem since it retains a jump overcall of 3♣ as a natural bid, but it is not always immediately specific about which minor is held in a major-minor two suiter.

♠ A Q 10 4 3   ♥ 3   ♦ A J 10 5 4 2   ♣ 8
and
♠ K 10 8 5 3 2   ♥ 3   ♦ A Q 9 7 4   ♣ 9

are typical Quantum bids after an opening bid of 1♣ or 1♥. The second hand is more suitable non-vulnerable, because of the lack of substance of either of the suits. Some of the time the hand will be a misfit, and there is a great deal of difference between a trump suit of K-10-8-5-3-2 and K-J-10-9-5-3 opposite a singleton. A Quantum bid promises a minimum of 5-5 in the two suits and shows potential playing strength, not defensive values.

♠ 6 5   ♥ K Q J 9 4 2   ♦ K Q 10 9 3   ♣ —

is a full strength Quantum at any vulnerability. If partner is considering doubling a high level contract in clubs or spades, visualising a hand such as this might dampen his ardour.

Quantum

After 1♣:	2♣	—	shows diamonds and spades
	2NT	—	shows diamonds and hearts
	3♣	—	shows hearts and spades
After 1♦:	2♦	—	shows clubs and spades
	2NT	—	shows clubs and hearts
	3♦	—	shows hearts and spades
After 1♥:	2♥	—	shows spades and a minor
	2NT	—	shows the minors
After 1♠:	2♠	—	shows hearts and a minor
	2NT	—	shows the minors

After 1♥ - 2♥ and 1♠ - 2♠ the response of 2NT asks partner to bid his minor. The way to remember Quantum is: cue-bid, extremes; no-trumps, lower suits; jump cue, majors.

It should be remembered that Quantum is a limit bid, and a response to it is also a limit bid.

1♠	2♠	Pass	3♥

Though there is an inference that partner has some heart support since he made no attempt to discover a minor suit fit, the bid of 3♥ denies the ability to bid game. The Quantum bidder proceeds at his own risk, for his partner may have no useful values. Similarly:

1♠	2♠	Pass	2NT
Pass	3♦	Pass	3♥
Pass	?		

Proceed with caution, the fact that the opponents have not bid means nothing, partner may have nine or ten black cards.

After 1♣ - 2♣ - Pass, and 1♦ - 2♦ - Pass, a bid of 2♥ is natural, and shows a suit at least as good as partner's suits. It would be unwise to introduce anything other than a semi-solid suit at the three level when partner announces the other two suits, but if it happens the bid is natural.

The Passed Hand

A two suiter not strong enough to open the bidding might be quite prepared to contest the part-score. Such a hand occurred in the heats of the 1979 Rothman's Simultaneous Pairs, and as a result of this hand, one pair who would otherwise have qualified, failed to do so:

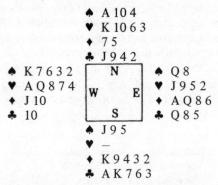

```
                    ♠ A 10 4
                    ♥ K 10 6 3
                    ♦ 7 5
                    ♣ J 9 4 2
        ♠ K 7 6 3 2    N       ♠ Q 8
        ♥ A Q 8 7 4            ♥ J 9 5 2
        ♦ J 10      W     E    ♦ A Q 8 6
        ♣ 10           S       ♣ Q 8 5
                    ♠ J 9 5
                    ♥ —
                    ♦ K 9 4 3 2
                    ♣ A K 7 6 3
```

Game in hearts, failing to make, and doubled at some tables, was a common result which is likely to happen if West considers that he has the values for an opening bid; in fact a plus score for East-West is a good result.

At the table in question the bidding was:

South	West	North	East
—	Pass	Pass	Pass
1♦	1NT	Pass	2♥
All Pass			

The bid of 1NT was alerted and explained as unusual, and on being pressed East said he thought it showed the lower suits, in this case clubs and hearts. At the conclusion of the play of the hand North-South claimed that they had been given misleading information and complained to the tournament director to that effect. The theoretical TNT of eighteen was borne out by some pairs having made ten tricks in clubs, and 2♥ made by East-West was a top score. The director upheld the claim and awarded an average minus to East-West. An appeal was made to the referee who rejected it on the grounds that though a wrong bid cannot incur a penalty, a wrong explanation of partner's bid may entail forfeiting a good result. It is ironical that if East decides to be unhelpful and insists that his partner's bid is undefined, or that he cannot remember, his conduct is unimpeachable; and if he is obliged to elaborate as to how he intends to treat his partner's bid, an answer such as, 'I'm going to bid my longest suit and see what happens', is ethically dubious but technically beyond reproach. Perhaps there is some poetic justice in this situation, for if West puts down his hand and upbraids his partner for forgetting the system, although he may not realise it, his discourtesy to his partner automatically prejudices his cause, whereas if he remarks, 'Sorry partner, I've got hearts and spades, I hope it won't matter', his opponents will thereafter have no legal grounds for complaint.

The conventional aids without which it is impossible to achieve a good result on this particular hand must be explicitly understood and explained. An overcall by a passed hand which cannot be natural shows a two suited hand. At favourable vulnerability, if fourth hand opens one of a major, two of the same major would certainly show a Quantum overcall, but at any other vulnerability it is not practical to force partner to the three level, and nothing neat can be achieved.

When fourth hand opens one of a minor there is more scope for adventure:

After 1♣:   2♦ — shows the majors
              2♣ — diamonds and spades
             1NT — shows diamonds and hearts

These bids are analogous to Quantum, where the most expensive bid shows the majors, the cue-bid shows the extremes, and no-trumps shows the two lower suits.

If the opening bid is 1♦ only two conventional bids are available, and these are used in such a way that partner is not forced to the three level:

After 1♦:   2♦ — shows the majors
            1NT — shows clubs and hearts (the lower suits)

A black two suiter is not catered for, and must either overcall 1♠ or double. As a logical reminder it is more dangerous to double with clubs and hearts than clubs and spades.

A slightly different situation arises when third or fourth hand opens one of a suit which is passed round to the protective position. Over a major suit 1NT should be a natural protective bid. When the suit is a minor two factors militate against a natural bid of 1NT; since partner could so easily have overcalled he is correspondingly less likely to have any useful values, and perhaps more important, one of a minor passed out is so often a silly contract that if it does not look right to double, it is probably wrong to bid a protective 1NT. For these reasons a partnership may decide to use two suited overcalls by the passed hand in a protective position.

The unusual no-trump

To enter a competed auction with a bid in no-trumps is unusual unless defined otherwise.

       1♣   Pass   1♠   2NT

A bid of 2♣ by fourth hand would have been competitive, looking for the magic eight-card fit at the two level. 2NT, forcing the bidding to the three level is a genuine Quantum bid in the red suits, guaranteeing five cards in each red suit and at most five losers, and acts as a limiting factor on the strength of the bid of 2♣.

The level of the introduction of no-trumps is largely a tactical consideration. The higher the bid the more sacrificial its nature. This is a standard principle of pre-emption, whereby, after the bidding: 1♣ - Pass - 1♠, a bid of 3♥ would show a strong jump overcall, but 4♥ would be more pre-emptive, and would have more hearts and less high cards. Similarly, after: 1♣ - Pass - 1♠ a butt in of 3NT is more sacrificial than 2NT, and if the bidding starts: 1♣ - Pass - 2♠, overcalls of 2NT, 3NT, or 4NT are a reflection of the scoring and vulnerability.

Two suiters after an opening bid of one no-trump

Bidding theory can develop in two ways. The empirical approach is to consider a problem which arises in the bidding and think what can be done about it. The theoretical approach uses idle bids, assigning meanings to the most unlikely bids that partner could possibly make. What does it mean if partner opens five of a major? No problem. Eleven tricks missing the ace and king of trumps. That it is odds against such a hand occurring outside a text book within any given decade is immaterial because the idea is incontrovertible in theory. This theoretical approach should not be despised for many good ideas have sprung from it, but one of its least brilliant products is the 2NT overcall of 1NT to show an unspecified two suiter. By the time that both suits have been shown the bidding will probably be at the four level, therefore the bid is game forcing, therefore it shows a three loser hand, something like 6-6-1-0 distribution. If you are of a cynical turn of mind and do not believe that you have held your fair share of this type of hand recently, you can reassure yourself that such hands do exist by looking in a text book.

A practical use of 2NT over 1NT must permit fit finding at the three level, and must also relate to the normal partnership defence against 1NT. Kelsey is as good as any and better than most at pairs scoring. Both 2♣ and 2♦ show three suited hands not strong enough to double, with a singleton or void, or sometimes a doubleton when nobody is looking. 2♣ shows a shortage in a red suit, 2♦ a shortage in a black suit. With moderate values correct to the corresponding major and go for the better part-score, with the proviso that if you are correcting 2♣ to 2♠, bid a red suit on the way in case he likes it.

The convention finds fairly sensible fits at the two level, and prevents the opponents from playing 1NT too often.

With Kelsey as the basic defence to 1NT a red two suiter can overcall 2♦, a black two suiter 2♣. Without Kelsey a black two suiter and a red two suiter must be described by bidding 3♣ and 3♦ respectively, at the cost of the natural bid. It is only possible to handle four of the six two suiters and be certain of stopping at the three level on minimum values. Once the fit can be found at the three level 2NT can be bid on the more common Quantum hand with four or five losers.

Responder first decides whether or not he has a good hand. In this context a flat hand with two aces is a very good hand because a fit is guaranteed, but if responder has two five-card suits headed by the king, the hand is a potential misfit. With a poor hand responder will bid 3♣, and this will normally be passed if clubs is one of partner's suits. If the overcaller does not hold clubs he will bid 3♦ to show diamonds and spades, or 3♥ to show the majors, and responder will pass, correct to the other suit, or bid game on fitting values.

So far this appears fool-proof, and there is no reason to go beyond the three level without either a good fit or sufficient high cards. But a hand did occur in a pairs event which created something of a problem:

♠ 5   ♥ A Q J 8 7 6   ♦ 10   ♣ A K 9 5 4

| 1NT (12-14) | 2NT | Pass | 3♣ |
| Pass | ? | | |

The player reasoned that his partner probably had some values, and if game in hearts was on, 3♣ could not be a good score. The difficulty was that a bid of 3♥ would show the majors, and might be corrected to 4♠. So the solution was to bid 4♥. This was smartly doubled. The full deal was:

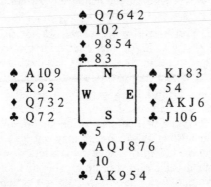

Since the clubs were breaking evenly there was no defence, and South had a lucky result. Two points emerge from this hand, the obvious one being the power of a two suiter provided it is not a misfit. Less obviously, if third hand passes 2NT it is a mistake to assume his hand is weak. Why should he double a forcing bid and warn his opponents? From his point of view it is far better to give them enough rope to hang themselves. He was very unlucky not to defeat 4♥ with the values he held, especially since 3NT was on for his side.

The second type of hand that responder can have is a weak hand with no club support, either a flat hand with a doubleton club, or some sort of shapely hand with a singleton club. He knows that there is a better fit than clubs. The response is 3♦, which does not promise any values. This response can be passed or corrected to 3♥ or 3♠. 3♠ would show a diamond-spade hand which is worth another try, 3♥ would show a heart suit, and might hold either black suit. Normally if responder bids 3♦ he will pass 3♥ or raise to 4♥, but note the sequence:

1NT	2NT	Pass	3♦
Pass	3♥	Pass	3♠

As in all of these sequences responder is not bidding suits of his own, he is trying to find his partner's suits. When he bids 3♦ he must have visualised the possibility of a heart-club hand opposite. Since he has no heart tolerance he must have positive values to bid this way. If the overcall does not contain spades he will convert 3♠ to 3NT, and responder may consider this playable or run to 4♣.

When responder has positive values sufficient to accept a game he has two alternative courses of action. Either he can start the fit finding procedure at the four level by bidding 4♣ or 4♦ or else he can bid 3NT to show a flat hand with general values. 3NT may be passed or converted to four of a major; and 4♣ over 3NT will show a minor two suiter not suitable for 3NT, such as:

♠ J 6   ♥ –   ♦ K Q J 9 4   ♣ K Q 10 8 7 3

If partner has ten or eleven points this hand is not going to make nine tricks in no-trumps; 4♣ will describe the hand well, partner may pass or raise either minor.

The only remaining possibility for responder is a one suited hand where the suit is at least as strong as his partner's suits. He can show this type of hand by bidding a major suit directly over 2NT and the bid will be passed or raised, or he can bid and rebid a good six- or seven-card minor.

With this 2NT overcall third hand may find himself in an unfamiliar situation which he has not discussed with his partner. He may bid for a variety of reasons. With values he may pass or he may double; he may bid a suit intending it as competitive or forcing; he may bid 3NT either on values or a long minor hoping his bid will terminate the auction. Whatever he does will not embarrass fourth hand who is quite capable of taking action at the four level if necessary. Should he choose to take no action, the Quantum bidder will bear this in mind if he is considering bidding again on his own initiative.

Although it may be a bluff, double by third hand is more likely to be made on values, and the defending side should go for immediate clarification. When the double runs round the two suiter will bid 3♥ to show the majors, 3♦ to show diamonds and spades, 3♣ to show clubs and hearts, and redouble for the minors. Conventional bids which might be forgotten should be shunned as the plague, the aide memoire here is that the higher the bid the higher ranking are the suits. Thus 3♣ is higher than redouble and the suits rank higher.

If third hand bids a suit, assuming it is not a psyche which would be very dangerous for his side, fourth hand immediately knows that his partner holds the other suit of the same colour:

1NT	2NT	3♥	3♠

The 2NT bid is marked with diamonds and one of the black suits, the bid of 3♠ is not a suit, but an effort to strike partner's black suit.

If the third hand bids 3NT, fourth hand may start finding operations at the four level, particularly at favourable vulnerability where three down will show a profit against a vulnerable game.

The passed hand overcalls against 1NT

Pairs contests are not won by allowing the opponents to play 1NT too often. The two suiter needs to overcall or protect. A black or red two suiter can conveniently bid 2♣ and 2♦ respectively. A major or minor two suiter can double, and partner will bid his better minor which will be corrected to 2♥ if the double was based on the majors. Playing weak twos in the majors it cannot make sense to protect 1NT with two of a major if the hand has already passed, therefore this bid should show a major minor two suiter of different colours.

Redouble of a conventional overcall

An understanding which can be valuable in conjunction with conventional bids to describe two suiters is the following: If the conventional overcall is doubled a redouble should be obligatory by a responding hand which holds a singleton in one of partner's suits and at least sound support for the other suit. If the bidding proceeds:

1♥	2NT	Dble	4♦

it is likely that 4♦ is pre-emptive, but it could be bid with the intention of making, and from the point of view of making game in diamonds a singleton club would be invaluable. Equally if the opponents bid 4♥ the knowledge of a singleton club would deter the defenders from sacrificing if they knew that they could start with the ace of clubs and a club ruff, in fact they might even be able to double. Of course the singleton might be in either of the two suits, the two suited hand will bid the lower suit which may be corrected or raised to the appropriate level.

A hand from the Great Britain trials of 1979 would have lent itself well to these methods:

♠ 8 6 5	♥ A 9 7 4 2	♦ A 10 8 3	♣ 4
Pass	1♥	Pass	Pass
2NT	Dble	?	

Partner would bid 3♣ over the redouble, and a raise to 4♦ would now describe the hand well. It is not certain that partner would have made the slam try in spades which would have led to the cold slam in diamonds, but he would have bid the game which was not reached by the majority of the competitors.

It will have been noted that an alternative use of the redouble has already been proposed, namely to show one card preference for the higher ranking of the two suits. A partnership may decide for the sake of simplicity to adopt one method or the other, but in fact it is possible to get the benefit of both. The distinction should be that if partner has a weak hand with suits of unspecified lengths, redouble is suit preference; but if partner guarantees a four or five loser hand, or if two or more bids were available to show the same strength hand, redouble shows a singleton.

Examples

1♣	Pass	1♥	2♣
Dble	Rdble		

Both 1NT and 2♣ were available, the 2♣ bid being used to show better spades, therefore redouble shows a singleton, and also carries the inference that the hand belongs to the defending side.

1♣	Pass	1♠	2♣
Dble	Rdble		

Here 2♣ was the only bid for take-out, and partner could have a weak 6-4 in the red suits either way round, redouble is part of the escape mechanism.

1♥	Pass	2♦	2NT
Dble	Rdble		

Fourth hand guarantees at least ten black cards and at most five losers, the redouble shows a singleton in a black suit.

Chapter 21
Defence to a Strong Club

There are many conventional defences against a strong club, and the choice of which to adopt is less important than a proper understanding of what the defending side should be doing in the bidding. For any bid to be successful it must fulfil one of three aims:

1   Result in gaining the contract profitably
2   Indicate a damaging lead
3   Consume the opponents' bidding space

A bid which achieves none of these objectives is a bad bid for it gives information to the opponents, warning them of possible dangers and allowing them to judge the distribution of the unseen hands.

Of the three aims in bidding, the one most easily realised when the opponents have announced 40 per cent or more of the honour strength is the third. Bidding against a strong club is, or should be, defensive and obstructive, and it follows that a strong hand should pass 1♣ and compete on the second round of bidding.

Before suggesting any conventional aids, some general ideas will be considered. Players have been known to double a strong club to show the values for an opening bid and a club suit. There is little virtue in such a bid. The chances of outbidding the strong hand with the lowest ranking suit are slim; if a club lead would be damaging the opponents will often be able to arrange for the dangerous hand to be left on lead; and far from consuming the opponents' bidding space, responder has been offered two additional bids, pass and redouble, whose meaning a good partnership will have discussed.

There was a hand quoted earlier to illustrate the principle of TNT where the bidding started:

South	West	North	East
—	Pass	1♣	1♦
Pass	1♥	1♠	Pass

East's bid of 1♦, showing a red two suiter, gave South the opportunity to pass, which showed 0-3 points. With no further interference North-South bid to a speculative slam in spades, and West then decided to sacrifice in 7♦. The fact that this bidding occurred in the 1979 final of Crockford's shows that even good players are capable of adopting inferior tactics through not having considered the philosophy behind their bids. Descriptive low level bids against the balance of strength are only acceptable on the understanding that partner will be able to raise the bidding to an inconvenient level on a fair percentage of deals. On the occasions when partner is unable to make a pre-emptive barrage the attack has aborted. By this criterion, the random spade overcall, illegal in this country, is of dubious merit.

The more bidding space which can be stolen from the opponents, the more desirable it is to bid, consistent with safety. Double, or 1♦, is destined to be an unlucky bid; 2♠ or 2NT, provided it escapes retribution, will be a lucky bid, forcing an error or posing an insoluble problem at least part of the time.

It is widely accepted that pre-empts are most effective when they contain an element of surprise. Thus it would be argued that to open 3♠ third in hand after two passes is more desirable than to overcall an opening bid of 1♣ with 3♠, and if the opponents have been able to open and respond before fourth hand has the opportunity to bid 3♠ the sting of the pre-empt has been lost. There is undeniable logic in this argument, but it is a mistake to conclude that: 1♣ - Pass - 1♥ - 3♠ is a lost cause. Even 2♠ in this sequence can be a rewarding sally; Blue Club players have to search for their fit at the three level, and Precision is robbed of the control asks and trump asks which Acol occasionally enjoys above the level of 4NT or 5NT. The argument that a weak jump to 2♠ is more effective when the response is 1♦ rather than 1♥ should also be viewed with suspicion. The opponents will be pleased to accept a penalty if they have no game on, but if they have announced game going values they will be less ready to settle for an inadequate penalty, and there is a further point that the defenders may be in doubt themselves whether the bid of 2♠ is serious or frivolous if the response is 1♦.

Finally and obviously, with regard to general principles, there is most to be gained by bidding a suit which is likely to outrank the opponent's suit. 2♠ courts the same penalty as 2♣ but causes more mischief.

Most conventional defences lean heavily on the principle that two suited hands can develop tricks even against the balance of points, and any defence is a compromise between retaining all major suit bids as natural and the desirability of expressing all six possible two suiters without ambiguity so that partner can make an immediate raise. The Truscott defence uses the bids ranging from double to 2♣ to describe two suiters: a minimum suit bid shows that suit and the suit above, double shows clubs and hearts, 1NT shows diamonds and spades. Disco gives precedence to 1♦, 1♥, and 1♠ being natural bids, and uses the remaining idle bids to describe two suiters as accurately as possible: double, the majors, 2♣ the black suits, 2♦ the reds, 2NT the minors, and regrettably but inevitably 1NT must describe two hands, the two non-touching two suiters.

If one is going to give up the option of expressing the two suiters un-unambiguously, there may be some merit in: 2♣ the reds, 2♦ the majors,

2NT the minors, and 1NT to show clubs and another suit. Then at least one suit is specified. The idea of bidding the suit below those held is that there may be an extra let out at the two level when the hand is a misfit, responder could pass a bid of 2♣ which showed the red suits, also he can redouble to show one card preference for the higher ranking suit if the artificial bid is doubled. A comprehensive schedule of suit below bids would use double and 1♦ to show non-touching two suiters, 1NT for the black suits, 2♣ for the reds, 2♦ the majors, and 2NT the minors.

Multi purpose bids against a strong club offer considerable scope for invention, but are not licensed in England. The Amsbury defence to 1♣ has a restricted licence and may only be played in national competitions: all suit bids at the one level are natural, double shows the majors, 1NT a non-touching two suiter, and 2NT the minors. Two level bids all have three possible meanings:

1   natural
2   a three suited hand where the singleton has been bid
3   a touching two suiter which does not include the suit which has been bid

Responder, if he wishes, can enquire about the hand type by bidding 2NT, then a simple rebid would indicate that the overcall was natural, a rebid in the suit ranking immediately below the suit already mentioned shows the three suited hand where the shortage was bid on the first round, and any other rebid would show a two suiter including the suit named and the next higher ranking suit. If the intervention is doubled and followed by two passes, redouble shows the three suiter, and any other rescue is the lower of the two touching suits. There is no doubt that this convention can be difficult to play against, and this is the chief criterion of an effective defence against a strong club.

Chapter 22
Transfers

Early in the history of the game it was realised that 2♣ in response to 1NT was better employed asking for four-card majors than as a natural weakness take-out. It was a long time before players drew the obvious conclusion that 2♦ as a natural weakness take-out was also a waste of time; certainly in the modern game if it were a good contract you would not be allowed to play it. The idea was born that 2♦ could be used as a transfer to 2♥, 2♥ to 2♠, and so on. There was an obvious advantage in opener playing the hand and having the lead coming up to his tenaces. But even more important, the transfer mechanism increased the number of bidding sequences which responder had at his disposal. 2♠, 2NT, 3♣, 3♦, 3♥, and 3♠ could all mean something different bid directly over 1NT than if they were preceded by the transfer to 2♥. The principle of transfers doubled the scope of bidding at the cost of one natural, rather inefficient sequence.

Players alive to the versatility of transfers will look for opportunities to use them in the contested auction. Suppose that your partner's bid of one of a major is overcalled by a conventional 2NT. If you hold the other major, say A-Q-J-x-x-x or K-Q-x-x-x-x-x and not much else, you are in an unenviable position. Pass may result in an easy game being missed, but if you bid there will be an innocent pass on your left, an ingenuous 3NT from partner, and the axe will descend from your left. The solution is to press 3♣ and 3♦ into service as conventional aids, and, of course, the most efficient method will involve transfers:

1 Three of partner's major is a TNT raise, and will show a hand similar to a raise to the three level over a take-out double. Partner is not invited to find the fourth, but on occasions will be delighted to do so.

2 Three of the other major is non-forcing, partner will pass or raise, and only bid 3NT at his own risk.

3 3♣ is a transfer to 3♦. Responder will then bid 3♥ to show a high card raise, or 3♠ forcing.

4 3♦ shows five cards in the other major and secondary support for partner's major. The hand will have at least ten or eleven high card points or equivalent distributional values. Opener is expected to bid game in no-trumps or either major if he can, responder may raise a three level rebid if he has values in reserve, and either player is free to cue-bid with slam interest.

Opponents will not necessarily be cowed into submission by the efficiency of these methods, and may be selfish enough to continue bidding in the minors. Opener will have no problems if his partner has bid three of either major, and will probably know what to do if the response was 3♦. Although the transfer of 3♣ shows the strongest values, it is nevertheless susceptible to interference. Opener will double to suggest penalties, bid diamonds over clubs at the four or five level to ask partner to declarer himself, and make a forcing pass over a bid in diamonds.

Responder will normally start by doubling 2NT if he has six or more minor suit cards, and doubles of the opponents' minor suit contracts will be according to the principle of consultative doubles. Any other auction is interpreted in the light of responder's failure to make one of the bids described above. For example:

1♠	2NT	Dble	3♣
Pass	Pass	3♥	

Since opener has not doubled 3♣ consultatively, responder is not prepared to double for penalties, he might have been prepared to take care of a diamond contract. He did not bid 3♦ on the first round, so he is unlikely to want to hear a rebid in spades. If he had a weak hand he would have bid 3♥ on the first round, but 3♥ cannot be forcing since he did not bid 3♣.

Low level transfers in the contested auction have an inherent defect. It is standard procedure to abandon transfers if 1NT is doubled, the over-riding necessity is to escape into a better contract which might be two of a minor. There are players who continue to use transfers by playing a redouble as a transfer to 2♣. The cost of the natural redouble is already a heavy price to pay for the pleasure of playing the hand the other way round. The unseen cost is greater. If third hand bids a natural 2♥, fourth hand will often have a difficult decision, and will have one opportunity to solve the problem. But if the bid is 2♦ as a transfer to 2♥ fourth hand immediately has a number of extra options; he can double to show diamonds, bid 2♥ as a weak take-out, pass (which many experts play as forcing) and then double for penalties, bid 2♠ to show a weak hand which would protect 2♥, or pass and bid 2♠ to show stronger values.

There can be a general danger in adopting new conventions without fully appreciating their strengths and weaknesses, and their effect on the opponents. When Joe Bloggs gets his name on a new convention he is unlikely to go to great lengths to explain the demerits of his brainchild to the world at large. It is more probable that his disciples will be left to discover these for themselves; and the real test of any convention is not how well it works against Mrs. Jones and Mrs. Brown who have never heard of it, but how well its works against players who have taken the trouble to devise counter measures. Low level transfers in the contested auction are best played by the opponents.

Lebensohl

If partner opens 1NT (12-14) and the next hand bids 2♠, you would like to bid 3♥ on:

♠ 7 5   ♥ A Q 9 7 4 2   ♦ Q 9 3   ♣ 8 3

and be allowed to play there.

If you held a stronger hand:

♠ 7 5   ♥ A Q 9 7 4 2   ♦ Q 9 3   ♣ A 8

you would like your bid of 3♥ to be forcing.

The Lebensohl convention performs this minor miracle with the aid of a transfer. 2NT is a command for opener to bid 3♣, then when responder continues with three of a suit this has a different meaning to an immediate three of a suit. It only remains to decide which is the stronger bid, 3♥ immediately, or 3♥ preceded by the transfer. The easy, obvious way is to say that three of a suit on the first round is forcing, since there is then no problem with a forcing 3♣ bid. But the easy obvious way is wrong because it reckons without the opposition, and this is always a mistake. Imagine:

1NT	2♠	2NT	3♠ or 4♠
?			

You have three cards in spades and two four-card suits outside. Partner has an unspecified six-card suit. If his six-card suit coincides with one of your four-card suits the TNT will be two higher than if you have a doubleton in his suit. Yet you cannot bid, you cannot double, you have been shut out of the auction. When the bid runs round to partner, he also is powerless, that is why he bid 2NT. Opponents sit back knowing their TNT raise must win whether the contract makes or not.

Responder must declare his suit with the weak hand; 2NT is the first move on a game force, and of course it is correspondingly less likely that the opponents will advance. It is possible to show a forcing 3♣ bid by transferring partner to 3♣, and then bidding 3NT. In practice, however, there is a better use for this sequence.

If 1NT is overcalled it can be difficult for the opening side to find a 4-4 major suit game. If the overcall is in a minor the problem is less acute since the cue-bid of the opponent's suit can serve to ask for the majors. When the overcall is in a major, the 4-4 fit in the other major can be lost. The following two rules were devised by the Sharples for use in conjunction with Lebensohl:

1   The cue-bid of the opponent's major shows four cards in the other major.

2   To go to game in no-trumps via 2NT denies a stop in the opponent's suit.

These two rules are most easily demonstrated by interpreting some sequences.

1NT	2♥	3♥

Responder has a raise to 3NT with a four-card spade suit.

1NT	2♥	2NT	Pass
3♣	Pass	3♥	

Again responder has four spades, but by bidding 2NT before cue-bidding 3♥ denies a stop in the opponent's suit. If opener bids 3NT without a stop he will lose the first five or six tricks. He can choose between playing a spade contract on a 4-3 fit, and looking for a 4-4 minor fit at the four-level.

1NT	2♥	2NT	Pass
3♣	Pass	3NT	

Responder denies a spade suit, he also denies a heart stop. Opener should run to four of a minor without a heart stop.

1NT	2♥	3NT

Responder has no spade suit, but he can stop hearts.

1NT	2♥	3♠

3♠ is invitational, with the normal weak Lebensohl hand he could have bid 2♠, and if he had wanted 3♠ to be forcing he would have bid 2NT first.

There is a further refinement which can be added to Lebensohl. 2NT is normally the first move on a strong hand and commands the bid of 3♣. If instead, opener is allowed to bid his better minor, none of the strong sequences are affected but responder can contest the part-score in the minors. Ideally he would have nine or ten minor suit cards, but at favourable vulnerability he might be prepared to chance his luck with two four-card minors and moderate values.

The price paid for all these Lebensohl sequences is the loss of the natural bid of 2NT. In view of what can be gained, the exchange is a bargain, but there are repercussions on the penalty double of an overcall. There are powerful voices to maintain that double should replace the natural 2NT, either with an invitational or with a competitive meaning. Other equally eminent authorities favour the retention of a penalty double. If double is not to be for penalties, possibly it is better played as a competitive manoeuvre imposing 2NT on the opening bidder, then any advance by responder opens up new vistas of possible interpretations. But let us hasten to add that it is not the policy here to advocate any convention which cannot amply justify its existence, and, in our view, double is best reserved for old fashioned penalties. Arguably the defences to 1NT are more efficient than the bid itself unless Lebensohl redresses the balance, and every effort should be made to deter the opponents from entering the auction. There must be strong reason for dispensing with the penalty double.

The overcall is conventional

Over the years there has been a succession of new conventional defences to 1NT, each one better than the last, or at least different. No doubt the trend will continue. In an international match an efficient non-playing captain would analyse the opponents' particular brand of interference and devise the best possible counter measures, and it could happen that there would be as many counter measures as there are conventions. Without the luxury of a conscientious non-playing captain, what is required is a simple effective method of combating interference which varies as little as possible from standard procedure.

For the purposes of playing against them, conventional overcalls can be divided into two types, those which have an anchor suit, and those which do not. The first group is least to be feared when the opening side holds the balance of strength. If 1NT is overcalled by two of a minor which guarantees hearts, the natural bid of 2♥ is no longer required, 2♥ becomes the strong Lebensohl bid, and responder has two extra bids at his disposal, double and 2NT.

With regard to the double, note the difference between:

	1NT	Dble	2♦ (transfer) Dble

and

	1NT	2♦ (transfer) Dble

In the first case fourth hand is delighted to be able to double to show five or six points and a diamond suit, partner's point count and distribution is undetermined and the double may enable him to take the right decision on the next round of bidding. In the second sequence there is no point doubling just to show diamonds; if the hand has diamonds but is not strong enough for a non-forcing bid of 3♦, it has no right to be bidding.

One use of the double is to show a consultative double of the opponent's anchor suit, with the understanding that an unequivocal penalty double will pass and double on the second round.

The fallacy of these methods is demonstrated by the hand below:

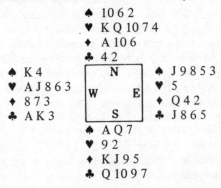

South	West	North	East
–	–	–	Pass
1NT	2♦	All Pass	

The bid of 2♦ was explained as showing hearts and possibly another suit. North found the trump lead and the contract went four off undoubled. 2♦ doubled would have cost 1100 and 2♥ doubled would not necessarily have fared any better.

The best defence against transfer overcalls is remarkably simple and foolproof. Double of the conventional overcall relates to the anchor suit, and shows either a consultative double, or a full-blooded penalty double. Three small trumps is not good enough for a double since opener will be very disappointed not to make a trump trick if he holds K-J-x. But any holding as good as J-x-x or better is sufficient for the double. Opener is expected to co-operate by doubling the escape with three or more cards in that suit, pass would show a doubleton. When opener does pass, showing a doubleton, responder will only double with a good trump holding; if he doubles with a three-card trump holding, at least he knows he is doubling an eight-card fit. Similar principles of consultation should apply regardless of how the opponents bid.

1NT	2♣ (hearts)	Dble	Pass
Pass	2♥	Pass	

Responder has three to an honour in hearts, but is not strong enough to double on his own initiative, opener should double, bid, or take a view and pass.

The cue-bid of the anchor suit will normally be a game force, but just as one weak type of hand previously crept into the Lebensohl 2NT bid, so here responder may employ the cue-bid on any hand where he is prepared to hear his partner rebid according to the schedule:

2♠ – a four-card suit
2NT – no spades, even length in the minors
3♣/♦ – the better minor, no spade suit

A hand such as:

♠ J 8 3 2   ♥ 4   ♦ K J 5 4 2   ♣ A 10 7

would cue-bid rather than hazard 3♦, and in view of the frequency of this type of hand as opposed to a forcing three of a minor, in the sequence:

1NT	2♦ (hearts)	2♥	Pass
2NT	Pass	3♣ or 3♦	

responder's bid should not be considered as forcing, he is merely running to his better minor. Similarly:

1NT	2♦	2♥	Pass
2♠	Pass	2NT	

asks for opener's better minor.

This only leaves responder's immediate bid of 2NT. Since an invitational 2NT could double first, the bid should be treated as competitive. Taking into account the hands which have already been eliminated, there is a strong suggestion that the hand does not contain four spades or three hearts. Opener can pass, or run to three of a minor if he does not like the thought of a heart attack against no-trumps.

When the opponent's anchor suit is spades, double has exactly the same development, and 2♠ is Lebensohl showing either a strong hand or the minors. The most efficient use of 2NT is invitational guaranteeing four cards in hearts, opener bids 3♥, 3NT, 4♥, or passes. A 2NT bid without four hearts could double the conventional overcall and bid 2NT on the second round. Note that there is a difference in the immediate 2NT bid when the opponents have hearts and spades. The reason for this is that when the opponents have hearts it is possible to locate a 4-4 spade fit via Lebensohl and stay in a part-score, but the reverse is not true when they have spades.

The simplest system of counter measures against a fit finding overcall which has no specific requirements other than some support for the bid minor is to treat it as a natural bid, doubling with general values and expecting partner to double any escape with a three-card holding or better. Here the general philosophy is to risk doubling two of a minor on the balance of points, but not to risk doubling an eight-card major fit.

If the overcall shows the majors, the double should have some defence against the majors, and again partner will double on three cards.

Defending against weak twos

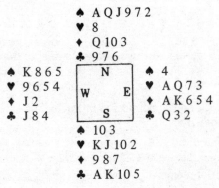

♠ A Q J 9 7 2
♥ 8
♦ Q 10 3
♣ 9 7 6

♠ K 8 6 5   ♠ 4
♥ 9 6 5 4   ♥ A Q 7 3
♦ J 2   ♦ A K 6 5 4
♣ J 8 4   ♣ Q 3 2

♠ 10 3
♥ K J 10 2
♦ 9 8 7
♣ A K 10 5

Room 1	South	West	North	East
	–	–	2♠	3♣ (i)
	Dble (ii)	Pass	Pass	3♦ (iii)
	Pass (iv)	Pass	Pass (v)	

(i) Weak take-out
(ii) A trap pass can be passed out
(iii) Did not fancy it in spite of his partner's pass
(iv) Later South thought his partner should have doubled
(v) North also thought his partner should have doubled

Room 2	South	West	North	East
	–	–	2♦ (i)	Pass (ii)
	2♥ (iii)	Pass	2♠	Dble (iv)
	Pass (v)	3♥	Pass	4♥ (vi)
	Dble	All Pass		

(i) Multi
(ii) Many players would prefer to bid 2♥ to show a take-out of spades
(iii) Technically incorrect but raises interesting possibilities
(iv) Weak take-out
(v) The trap pass is easier to find when the take-out bid is double
(vi) If partner had a five-card heart suit to the king and the king of clubs it would be wrong to pass

At both tables the ten of spades was led and overtaken by the jack. The card play was good in both rooms and both contracts were three off.

The hand offers a good illustration of how points are won and lost in top class bridge without players making demonstrable mistakes. It would be invidious to attempt to assign the blame for North-South's failure to double 3♦ in Room 1. Without prior discussion, this sort of situation is difficult. Ideally South would not double 3♣ unless he had good defensive prospects against other three level contracts, and that being the case perhaps North should double 3♦. But even if 3♦ is doubled, West can still win 300 points on the board by running to 3♥, all because of what has happened in the other room. It is in the other room that the points have been lost, since game on the East-West cards is a very poor proposition. No doubt the methods employed by East-West would be satisfactory on nine deals out of ten, but on this deal they have been proved inadequate. It is a depressing feature of the top class teams game that credit is more easily lost than gained, and if anyone earns credit on this deal it must be South in Room 2. If he bid 2♥ because he only has eleven points, the only credit he can justly claim is for sitting in the right place at the right time when 800 was about to fall into his lap. On the other hand if he bid 2♥ in the hope that the opponents will commit an indiscretion when his partner has a weak two in spades, he is to be applauded.

The reason for presenting this hand is to plead the case for transfers when defending against weak twos. It is essential to have a weak and a strong take-out against weak twos. If the take-out promises thirteen points upwards and a minimum response can show 0-10 points, sensible contracts will only be reached by the grace of God and the help of the opposition.

The advantage of playing a double of 2♥ as weak take-out is that partner is not obliged to go beyond 2♠. If it is accepted that the double of 2♠ is also for take-out, which should not be granted without due consideration, then transfers are almost obligatory. Responder will seldom want to play for eight tricks in no-trumps; the success of a no-trump contract will usually depend on the unpredictable, whether the spade suit has a certain outside entry. If responder wants to play no-trumps he may as well bid three and have done with it. 2NT is a transfer to 3♣, doubling responder's range of expression.

If the opponents' methods allow them to bid again in spades after an auction has started: 2♠ - Dble - Pass, they are unlikely to cause any great anguish to the defending side. For all practical purposes the opening side has been silenced other than to double the final contract. For this reason 2NT shows the weak hand. After the bidding:

2♠	Dble	Pass	2NT
Pass	3♣	?	

the hand which is lying in ambush must now double on the knowledge that his left hand opponent has a weak hand with an unspecified five- or six-card suit, or a flat Yarborough, or a hand which is about to redouble for the red suits. If he is going to catch a little fish, he has to be clever and lucky, for the fish is very slippery.

If the third hand redoubles, the continuations must not depend on whether the redouble shows spades or denies them, some opponents will endeavour to get the best of both worlds. Pass from fourth hand asks partner to bale himself out, 2NT means what it did before, and three of a suit can be raised by a maximum weak take-out.

Chapter 23
The Forcing Pass

To a beginner a forcing pass is a very rare occurrence.

2♣ (Acol)	2♥	2♠	4♥
Pass	Pass	?	

An inexperienced responder might be rather bemused, he would wonder if the opponents were pulling his leg, he might suspect that his partner had psyched, and he might even pass on the assumption that if his partner could not double then neither could he since he had stretched to bid 2♠ anyway. In the beginners' game the forcing pass would be even more unlikely to occur since opener would not pass. He would subside into an agonised trance, wondering whether to double, bid 4♠, or put a toe on five of a minor. It would never occur to him that he could effectively do all three things simply by passing.

Although the forcing pass is used frequently in expert circles to avoid taking unilateral decisions where partner may be better placed to judge, there is little agreement amongst the experts themselves as to the exact nature of a forcing pass, and any reference in books is couched in vague general terms. The subject is controversial and for the most part uncharted.

Let us start with an uncontroversial sequence:

1♥	1♠	4♥	4♠

Few, if any, experts would maintain that a pass by opener is forcing. Either opener or responder is free to double or bid on, but if opener does neither, responder is not obliged to bid unless he considers that it is a mathematically sound proposition to do so. Now assume that either opener or responder does advance to 5♥, and 5♠ comes up. Does it have to be doubled? If so, why? Has the opening side not gained sufficient advantage by forcing the opponents to the five level, or do they have to write down −850 or −1050 if the hand is a freak?

Consider this group of sequences:

1♥	2♠	4♥	4♠
1♥	Dble	4♥	4♠
1♥	3♠	4♥	4♠
1♥	2♥ (2 suiter)	4♥	4♠

Opener and responder have shown the same values as in the sequence:

1♥	1♠	4♥	4♠

the only alteration is that the opponents have arrived at their contract via a different route. Their honour strength and trump length may be divided differently. Their values may vary according to their system and vulnerability. But the critical factor is what you and your partner have promised, and that remains the same. This principle may be formulated as follows:

Rule A   The opponents' methods of arriving at their contract is irrelevant to the forcing pass.

Already we run into trouble. According to the Bridge Players' Encyclopedia, 'A forcing pass may be made when the opponents have made an obvious sacrifice'. Excellent. Who would quarrel with such an authoritative, self-evident statement? Yet it makes nonsense of Rule A. This glib statement overlooks the fact that it will not always be obvious when they are sacrificing. Even if it is obvious to one player it may not be obvious to his partner. Take an example: Colonel Blimp overcalls 1♠, and bids one more spade every time the bidding comes round to him until he eventually arrives in 4♠. Must he be doubled? The answer lies not in the way the good colonel has bid his hand, but in the values that opener and responder have shown in the bidding. If the Unlucky Expert doubles merely because he does not like the way the hand has been bid, he will find either that Colonel Blimp has ample justification for his final bid, or that dummy is disgustingly suitable, for Colonel Blimp's partner knew that there was no need to enter the bidding.

Consider the following sequence:

1♦	1♠	2♣	2♠
3♣	3♠	Pass	Pass
4♣	Pass	Pass	4♠

Is it obligatory that opener or responder should double the opponents? Obviously their bidding does not sound strong. But doubling on the sound of the bidding, or worse still trapping partner into doubling unwillingly, is a recipe for disaster. The opponents may be weak players who have stumbled into a good contract in spite of themselves, or they may be experts playing a deep game. Of course, 4♠ has the appearance of a sacrifice. But if it is an obvious sacrifice, the player to whom it is obvious should double. The opponents' method of arriving in 4♠ is not what determines whether or not they must be doubled. The only relevant question is whether an opening bid and a response at the two level are sufficient in themselves to warrant doubling the opponents.

The most improbable illustrations of any theory are always from actual play. The one that follows is no exception. Study this bidding sequence and estimate how much the sacrifice will cost:

1♦	Pass	2♠	Pass
3♥	Pass	4NT	5♣
5♦	6♣	6♠	Pass
Pass	7♣	Pass	Pass
Dble	All Pass		

Responder's forcing pass was explained by the fact that DOPI and DOPE had never been discussed, and it was not clear how many aces 5♦ showed.

The ace of diamonds was not the happiest of leads, since the full deal was:

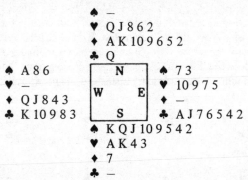

There is no doubt that the pass of 7♣ is forcing. In fact if there is such a thing as a bid which is 90 per cent forcing, the logical corollary is that this bid is 110 per cent forcing. The hand provides a fine illustration of how much credence should be placed on the opponents' bidding. They are not there to demonstrate the infallibility of your bidding methods.

Rule B   The values you have shown in reaching your contract determine whether a subsequent pass is forcing.

1♥	1♠	2♠	4♠

Many players would treat a pass by opener as forcing. To some extent it depends on the definition of the cue-bid. According to the treatment recommended previously, whereby 2♠ shows at least an invitational raise to 3♥, it does not necessarily follow that responder will have a stronger hand than if he had bid 4♥, and the pass should not be forcing. It is more likely that 4♠ will be doubled here than when responder made a direct raise in hearts, but that is not the same thing as saying the pass is forcing. It is not a question of getting it right most of the time, it is more a question of avoiding silly misunderstandings. Does opener's pass show a very weak hand or a very strong hand? What a horrible situation if pass would be forcing and opener has:

♠ Q 7   ♥ A K J 8 3   ♦ Q 7 6   ♣ J 8 2

Not only a nasty technical problem, but also a severe test in ethics!

Consider the difference between the following two sequences:

1♥	1♠	3♥	3♠
4♥	Pass	Pass	4♠
Pass			

and

1♥	1♠	3♥	3♠
4♣	Pass	4♥	4♠
Pass			

In the first sequence opener's pass is not forcing. Most experts would agree, however, that it is forcing in the second sequence. In an uncontested auction the bid of 4♣ would be a slam try. So it is in this contested auction, unless it is defined otherwise. If opener is prepared to make a slam try, he is prepared to underwrite 5♥, and the pass now tells responder to either bid 5♥ or double 5♠, whichever he finds least distasteful. He is not allowed to pass.

By analogy:

1♥	1♠	4♥	4♠
5♥	Pass	Pass	5♠
Pass			

and

1♥	1♠	4♥	4♠
5♣	Pass	5♥	5♠
Pass			

are different. Perhaps it is possible to argue that 5♣ is not a slam try, that it merely suggests a club rather than a heart lead if the opponents bid 5♠. But an excuse can always be made for faulty theory or bad judgment. The bid of 5♣ carries with it the assumption that the opponents will not be allowed to play in 5♠ undoubled. Whether opener is right to pass to his reluctant partner the decision of bidding 6♥ or doubling 5♠ is open to question, but there is no doubt that responder must do one or the other.

Rule C   A forcing pass must be clearly understood and respected as such on the merits of the sequence, without regard to either hand.

Experts have been known to describe a bid as 90 per cent forcing. That is an abuse of language, and a contradiction in terms. If you open 1♥ first in hand on a flat Yarborough and pass the response of 2♠, it is up to you to make your peace with partner after the dust has settled. 2♠ was forcing. What is meant by 90 per cent forcing is that the bid is highly encouraging and will only be passed if partner has an unusually poor hand. To regard a forcing pass in this light is defeating the object of the exercise. If opponents have bid to an annoyingly high level and you have reserves of strength, what is left for partner except a poor hand? Yet he must not pass.

Pass (forcing) as an answer to a bidding problem is no answer at all unless it is demonstrably clear from the bidding sequence that such a pass must be forcing. That a bidding problem can only be solved by a forcing pass does not make the pass forcing from partner's side of the table.

There are some doubles in low level competitive auctions which are ambiguous.

1♣	Pass	1NT	Pass
2♣	Dble		

On paper the double is for penalties. Nevertheless some tournament players prefer to define such a double as ambiguous on the theory that partner will be able to judge from his club holding. Dangerous but playable. There can be no question of leaving partner to judge whether or not a pass is forcing, there will be nothing in his hand to guide him.

Having attempted to brush away the cobwebs that obscure this issue, let us pose the central question, what values already announced in the auction are sufficient to make a subsequent pass forcing? What about an opening bid and a response at the two level?

1♦	1♠	2♣	3♠
Pass			

or

1♦	1♠	2♣	4♠
Pass			

The opening side expect to hold the balance of the points, and will rarely let the opponents play undoubled. That, however, as has been shown, does not constitute a forcing pass. Now it would be possible to say that the opponents will so seldom be allowed to win the contract undoubled that it will gain more than it loses in the long run to play a forcing pass here. If opener has:

♠ K 8   ♥ 7 3   ♦ A K J 9 4 3   ♣ J 5 3

and responder has:

♠ 9 3   ♥ Q 4   ♦ Q 7 5   ♣ K Q 10 9 7 2

and responder is forced to double and write down 4♠ doubled + 2, he may console himself that it will not happen very often. But the thought of it happening at all is not very appealing, and the recommended method is that an opening bid and a response at the two level are not sufficient. After: 1♦ - 1♠ - 2♣ - 4♠, opener will double if he can, or bid if he can, but if he does neither, the pass is not forcing and responder is not honour bound to re-enact the Charge of the Light Brigade.

There is an added complication in this particular sequence. If pass by opener is not forcing, what is to be done with a good hand that cannot choose between 5♣ and 5♦? Strong club players will gladly forego Blackwood here, and bid 4NT, whereas Acol players will be more reluctant to abandon their Blackwood. But to argue that pass is forcing because 4NT is Blackwood, is a case of the tail wagging the dog.

There is no agreement amongst experts, it a question of taking a stand, and the stand taken here is Rule D:

Rule D   If opener and responder have shown game going values before agreeing a fit, a subsequent pass is forcing.

Compare:

1♥	1♠	2NT	Pass
3♣	3♠	Pass	

and

1♥	1♠	2NT	3♠
Pass			

In the first sequence the final pass is forcing, in the second it is not. 3♣ is game forcing according to standard methods, responder has no heart preference, only a modest spade stop, by inference some club support, and is giving opener the choice of defending; 3♠ cannot be played undoubled. In the second sequence, responder will often double, but he is not obliged to, opener should have found a bid if he could.

2NT	Pass	Pass	3♥
Pass			

The pass is not forcing. Why should opener double with only one ace and a doubleton heart? Is the possession of twenty points massed in one hand enough to double the enemy at the three level? Opener has not doubled because he does not want to. Responder is free to double if he wishes.

2NT	3♥	3♠	4♥

The pass is forcing. 4♥ doubled may yield more than 4♠, or it may offer a more certain plus score.

2NT	Pass	3♥	3♠
Pass			

Forcing. If 3NT or 4♥ is not obvious, then pass must be correct. Partner will be better placed to judge whether to double, bid 3NT or 4♥, or even introduce another suit.

2NT	Pass	3♥	3♠
4♥	4♠	Pass	

Again the pass is forcing. The opening side has shown game going values before agreeing a fit. The bidding of the opponents falls under the heading of 'obvious' sacrificing. The forcing pass is used to avoid taking an inadequate penalty or doubling a sacrifice which is making.

This definition of game going values has the merit of being clear and concise, and prevents silly misunderstandings, such as the following which occurred in a high standard team of four match:

2NT	3♣	Pass	4♥
Pass	Pass	4♠	Pass
Pass	Dble	All Pass	

3♣ showed a two suiter including hearts. The contract was two down, because the player who doubled had a second suit of spades. Opener, to his credit, passed smoothly, reasoning that the opponents obviously wanted to be doubled, therefore he would not oblige, also he was a limited hand and partner was still there to employ the hatchet if necessary. The previous examples have shown that the fact that one hand is limited is merely one more red herring. Anyway that was not the way the sequence appeared from the other side of the table. 4♥ was so obviously a sacrifice that opener's only reason for passing with a good hand was a four-card spade suit. Experts sometimes create their own problems. In a lesser game opener would have hacked the opponents out of pique, and even if he had not, responder would never have exercised his judgment to the extent of bidding 4♠.

Rule E   The forcing pass operates at any level.

This is the simplest answer and the best. If you bid up to 7♥ and an opponent stumbles in with 7♠, pass shows the ace of spades and invites partner to bid 7NT; if he has already shown a spade guard in the bidding, and you have bid the grand with a void, then pass asks him for 7NT if his spade guard is the ace. At the other end of the scale, 1♣ - 1♥ is a game force in Precision; if an opponent overcalls 1♠, pass is open to interpretation, but one thing is certain. It is forcing. In Blue Club, after 1♣ - Pass 1♥ - 1♠ the most pressing need for double is for take-out, and pass is for penalties. Also in Blue Club, 1♣ - Pass - 1♥ - Dble, Pass shows hearts and is forcing to 2NT. Redouble also shows hearts but is game forcing.

There is a group of sequences where a player passes in the knowledge that an opponent's bid will be not be passed by partner. Though not conforming to the strictest definition of the forcing pass, they are, nonetheless, sufficiently similar to require mentioning.

1♥	Dble	Rdble	1♠
Pass			

The classical redouble denies a fit for partner's suit, guarantees the balance of the points even though partner may have opened light, and suggests that opener should leave further action to partner. By obeying instructions, opener has produced a pass which is forcing. It is generally accepted theory that if opener bids over 1♠ in this sequence he is showing a minimum hand, whereas if he passes first and then removes 1♠ doubled he shows a better hand. Though it might be possible to reverse the interpretation, the distinction is worth making.

The redouble of an opponent's take-out double can occur in a different form.

1♦	Pass	1♥	Dble
Rdble			

The redouble carries the same inference, the majority of the points, no obvious fit for partner, and a desire to penalise the opponents. Opener's hand will bear some resemblance to a 1NT or 2NT rebid; one obvious reason for preferring the redouble would be a singleton in partner's suit.

There was a bidding problem posed to a panel of experts which started with these five bids. The scoring was pairs and East-West were vulnerable.

South	West	North	East
Pass	Pass	1♦	Pass
1♥	Dble	Rdble	1♠
Pass	2♠	Dble	Pass
?			

South held:

♠ A K   ♥ Q 9 6 4 3   ♦ 7 4 3   ♣ 8 6 4

Only four experts out of fifteen voted for a pass, though in fact the pass would have brought in 800. One expert said that he did not see why it was necessary for North to double 2♠ when a pass would have been forcing. The forcing nature of a pass in this sequence is questionable. Partner has been advised not to try to describe his hand over 1♠, but now we are to believe that the pass of 2♠ countermands the previous instruction and commands partner to find a bid above the level of 2♠ regardless of how weak he is. That a pass here would be forcing has all the charm of the medieval ecclesiastical debate concerning the number of angels that could dance on the head of a pin. Only one thing is certain, no expert should inflict the sequence upon his bewildered partner.

This sequence provides a succinct final comment on the forcing pass. It is insufficiently used by weak players, and used too often by experts.

PART III

Psychology

Chapter 24
Believe the Improbable

'Son,' said the old guy, 'no matter how far you travel, or how smart you get, always remember this: Some day, somewhere,' he says, 'a guy is going to come to you and show you a nice brand-new deck of cards on which the seal is never broken, and this guy is going to bet you that the jack of spades will jump out of this deck and squirt cider in your ear. But, son.' the old guy says, 'do not bet him, for as sure as you do, you are going to get an ear full of cider.' (Damon Runyon)

East-West Game, IMPs, Dealer East

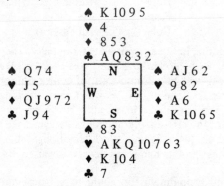

There does not appear to be anything improbable about this hand. East is likely to open, but South will probably play a part-score in hearts. That is not quite how things turned out at one table. After East's opening bid of 1NT, South decided that a jump bid in hearts would cause the opponents no trouble at all, and a double would only lead to a part-score in hearts, the prospect of defending a no-trump contract was more attractive. He passed. West bid 2♦ which was passed back to South. If the opponents could not rustle up anything more than 2♦ partner was marked with values, 3NT quoth South. West added his points to his partner's, and doubled indignantly. Redouble, said North, who could see his nine points quite clearly in spite of the poor lighting. The queen of diamonds was led to the ace and a diamond returned. In the four-card ending there was no defence to the overtrick. In desperation East blanked the ace of spades, and that was two redoubled overtricks.

Even good players base their bidding on the assumption that if they have the majority of the points the opponents cannot make anything. The main theme of this book is to show that point count is strictly for beginners.

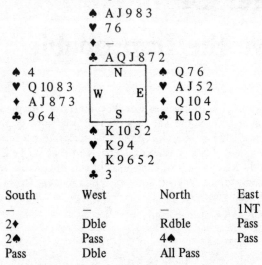

	♠ A J 9 8 3		
	♥ 7 6		
	♦ —		
	♣ A Q J 8 7 2		

	North	
West		East
♠ 4		♠ Q 7 6
♥ Q 10 8 3	W E	♥ A J 5 2
♦ A J 8 7 3		♦ Q 10 4
♣ 9 6 4	South	♣ K 10 5

	♠ K 10 5 2	
	♥ K 9 4	
	♦ K 9 6 5 2	
	♣ 3	

South	West	North	East
—	—	—	1NT
2♦	Dble	Rdble	Pass
2♠	Pass	4♠	Pass
Pass	Dble	All Pass	

The method of scoring has been omitted intentionally. There is no form of scoring whereby 4♠ doubled can be a good reuslt for East-West. West found the technically correct lead of a trump, but, of course, there was no way of preventing two overtricks. The bid of 2♦ was Kelsey showing a three suited hand with a shortage in one of the black suits. North has made a completely voluntary advance to 4♠, presumably he thinks he can make ten tricks. Has West any reason at all to disbelieve him? He thought the red suits were stacked against declarer, and he had seven points. Seven points!

On the next hand a complete top could have been won in a big pairs contest simply by believing that the opponents had some reason for bidding as they did.

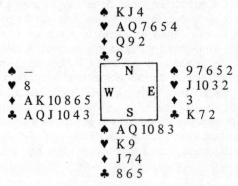

	♠ K J 4	
	♥ A Q 7 6 5 4	
	♦ Q 9 2	
	♣ 9	

	North	
West		East
♠ —		♠ 9 7 6 5 2
♥ 8	W E	♥ J 10 3 2
♦ A K 10 8 6 5		♦ 3
♣ A Q J 10 4 3	South	♣ K 7 2

	♠ A Q 10 8 3	
	♥ K 9	
	♦ J 7 4	
	♣ 8 6 5	

South	West	North	East
—	—	1♥	Pass
1♠	2NT	Pass	3♣
3♠	4NT (B'wood)	Pass	5♣
Dble	All Pass		

The universal result was a club contract doubled, either five or six. Black-wood may not be the ideal solution to West's problems, but all South had to do was believe that there was some reason for the bid, pass, and collect a top, provided his partner also realises that there is no cause to double.

On the last hand it is not difficult to refrain from doubling. The next hand is far more difficult; at love all you deal and open 1♦, holding:

♠ A 7   ♥ A J 9 7   ♦ A Q 8 5 3   ♣ J 3

Partner bids 1♥, you raise to 3♥, and he produces the fourth. You are all set to put dummy down when the next hand comes in with 4♠. There is no doubt that at the table ninety-nine players out of a hundred would double, which is precisely what happened. But can this be right? You have described your hand within narrow limits; pass, and let partner judge. It is a well-known ploy to pass as long as you dare on a freak hand, after all it would not be difficult for the opponent to pass over 1♦ - Pass - 1♥ with ten playing tricks in the black suits.

In the fact the full deal was far more instructive than a mundane ten play-ing tricks:

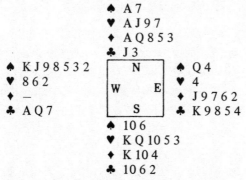

```
                    ♠ A 7
                    ♥ A J 9 7
                    ♦ A Q 8 5 3
                    ♣ J 3
  ♠ K J 9 8 5 3 2   ┌─────────┐   ♠ Q 4
  ♥ 8 6 2           │    N    │   ♥ 4
  ♦ —               │  W   E  │   ♦ J 9 7 6 2
  ♣ A Q 7           │    S    │   ♣ K 9 8 5 4
                    └─────────┘
                    ♠ 10 6
                    ♥ K Q 10 5 3
                    ♦ K 10 4
                    ♣ 10 6 2
```

The only lead to beat 4♠ is the seven of spades. Either ace and another spade, or the ace of hearts followed by ace and another spade gives an over-trick.

West has been lucky finding such a suitable dummy, but consider his first pass. Whether he bids 1♠, 2♠, 3♠, or 4♠, there is no way that he and his partner can be better placed than the opponents to judge the outcome of the hand. Partner might have values in hearts which will be ripped up by the opening lead. Opener could be sitting there with values in the black suits waiting to rebid 2NT, and the hand could be a total carnage in order to save against a very dubious game. The only solution to a hand such as this is to pass, listen to what the opponents have to say and apply the rules of total distribution and TNT.

The main theme of this chapter is believing the opponents. Assume that they are not lunatics until it is proved to be otherwise. If you open 1♠ and hear partner bid 2♦, you do not expect the next hand to come in with 6♣. Do not double on point count if it does happen, presumably he has some reason for bidding it. If you do double and lead the ace of diamonds, do not be surprised if it gets ruffed and declarer makes twelve tricks. Perhaps that is why he bid it.

Chapter 25
Give them Credit, but Not Too Much

The opponents will usually have some reason for making unlikely sounding bids. That was the theme of the previous chapter. But to assume that they will always make their contracts would be extremely pessimistic. At IMP scoring it is a sound proposition to bid games which are slightly odds against making. If these games run into bad breaks, with finesses wrong or adverse ruffs, they will not make, and may go two or even three off.

Game All, IMPs, Dealer East

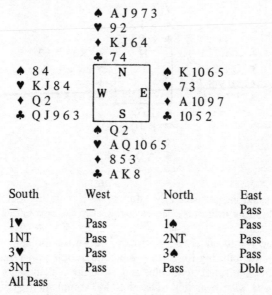

```
              ♠ A J 9 7 3
              ♥ 9 2
              ♦ K J 6 4
              ♣ 7 4
  ♠ 8 4           N           ♠ K 10 6 5
  ♥ K J 8 4                   ♥ 7 3
  ♦ Q 2       W       E       ♦ A 10 9 7
  ♣ Q J 9 6 3     S           ♣ 10 5 2
              ♠ Q 2
              ♥ A Q 10 6 5
              ♦ 8 5 3
              ♣ A K 8
```

South	West	North	East
—	—	—	Pass
1♥	Pass	1♠	Pass
1NT	Pass	2NT	Pass
3♥	Pass	3♠	Pass
3NT	Pass	Pass	Dble
All Pass			

The bidding is strictly limited, East knows that his partner has about an eight count, and that the cards are lying badly for declarer. To double in this sort of situation is referred to as 'diagnosing a double'. Partner may lead dummy's suit, but should prefer an unbid suit if that is his natural lead. On the actual hand West led the eight of spades, the nine of spades held the trick, and declarer established the hearts for one off. Against the natural lead of the queen of clubs declarer will make only six tricks.

To double when the opponents may have reserves of playing strength carries a different inference.

South	West	North	East
1♥	Pass	1♠	Pass
1NT	Pass	3NT	Dble
Pass	Pass	Rdble	All Pass

East has doubled, risking a redoubled overtrick in order to secure the most favourable lead from his partner. There is a modern convention which states that the player on lead should lead from his shorter holding in the unbid suits against this unlimited sequence. Without the dubious benefit of this convention one would tend to lead from the shorter minor with a useless hand if partner did not double, on the assumption that it is necessary to strike his most likely strength. But if he does double, this is a command to lead dummy's suit. When this auction occurred, West made no mistake, and the spade lead brought in a thousand points. On any other lead declarer can get home with the aid of a throw in:

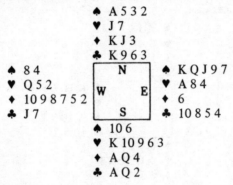

```
                    ♠ A 5 3 2
                    ♥ J 7
                    ♦ K J 3
                    ♣ K 9 6 3
     ♠ 8 4              N          ♠ K Q J 9 7
     ♥ Q 5 2                       ♥ A 8 4
     ♦ 10 9 8 7 5 2   W    E       ♦ 6
     ♣ J 7              S          ♣ 10 8 5 4
                    ♠ 10 6
                    ♥ K 10 9 6 3
                    ♦ A Q 4
                    ♣ A Q 2
```

When considering a speculative double it is wise to ascertain that the opponents' bidding is limited. Before strong club systems gained their present popularity a good player listened to the auction: 1♠ - 2♣ - 2♠ - 3♠ - 4♠, the 4♠ bid being produced after a noticeable pause for thought. He concluded that declarer was pushing for a thin game and doubled on a singleton trump. Opener found a prompt redouble, and rejecting a dangerous line of play, settled for one safe overtrick. The doubler complained that he had been conned by the opponent's pause. Opener, full of injured innocence, explained that he had been considering a slam try. This failed to satisfy the doubler in spite of soothing comments from his partner and from his team-mates who were watching, and the law was summoned. It was pointed out to the still agitated doubler that if he was not aware that the bid of 2♠ was forcing he was entitled to enquire, and if he chose not to do so he had no cause for complaint.

Occasional successes can be gained from doubling freely bid contracts, but often the effect of doubling with a trump stack is to warn declarer who goes one off instead of two and nothing is achieved. The really rich harvest from penalty doubles comes from the contested auction. When the auction is uncontested the opponents are bidding contracts which they think they can make. The same is not true of an auction such as: 1♥ - 1♠ - 4♥ - 4♠. 4♠ may be bid to make, or it may be bid as a sacrifice. If the distributional factor is working for the opponents and 4♠ is bid to make, the contract could make with an overtrick; if it is a sacrifice, it might be misjudged and could go four down.

Similarly, on:

1♥	2♣	3♥	4♣
4♥			

opener may have rejected a slam try, or he may be bidding game on very thin values because he does not wish to defend against 4♣. Perhaps he thought he could afford two off undoubled not vulnerable, to save against 130, in which case he may go three off. Anything is possible from two overtricks to three undertricks.

Just as important as technique is the philosophy of doubling. Some players give the impression of believing that all competitive auctions are rightly terminated by a double. Their lives are always interesting, and their score cards are no less so. Other players err in the opposite direction, believing that good teams play consists of avoiding loss, and to them −790 not only costs 5 IMP but also causes a loss in self esteem. That is the error of judgment that shows, the +150 which could have been converted to +500 with a timely double goes unnoticed. But the fact of the matter is that the player who prides himself on never writing down −790 is passing up opportunities of covering the cost of such accidents several times over.

The irony of penalty doubles is that those which appear most profitable seldom turn out that way. The sure-fire double has a habit of proving to be inadequate compensation for a missed game. It is the speculative double, when the opponents have stretched and lose trump control which brings in the points.

North-South Game, IMPs, Dealer West

South	West	North	East
—	1♣	Pass	1♥
4♦	4♥	?	

North holds:

♠ 86   ♥ A 10 9 5   ♦ J 7 6 3   ♣ A 6 5

The hand evaluates easily to three defensive tricks, and partner has a good suit of diamonds. Is it worth a double?

The full deal was:

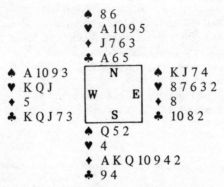

<pre>
                   ♠ 8 6
                   ♥ A 10 9 5
                   ♦ J 7 6 3
                   ♣ A 6 5
 ♠ A 10 9 3   ┌─────────┐   ♠ K J 7 4
 ♥ K Q J   │   N   │   ♥ 8 7 6 3 2
 ♦ 5   │ W   E │   ♦ 8
 ♣ K Q J 7 3   │   S   │   ♣ 10 8 2
                 └─────────┘
                   ♠ Q 5 2
                   ♥ 4
                   ♦ A K Q 10 9 4 2
                   ♣ 9 4
</pre>

Against repeated diamond forces, declarer lost trump control, misguessed the spades, and went five down. Only 250, because North did not double.

On a different occasion 250 was more difficult to convert to 900.

Love All, Dealer North

South	West	North	East
–	–	Pass	Pass
1♦	3♣ (Ghestem)	Dble	3♠
Pass	4♠	?	

North holds:

♠ 9 7 3   ♥ A 9 4   ♦ 7   ♣ A J 10 6 5 2

The Ghestem overcall showed the majors, and the double showed values rather than clubs. With the prospect of either a forcing game or some cheap ruffs, a double must be an acceptable risks. 3♠ was limited and 4♠ may have been ill judged. Just how ill judged it was, is revealed by the full diagram:

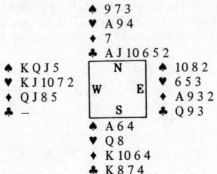

<pre>
                   ♠ 9 7 3
                   ♥ A 9 4
                   ♦ 7
                   ♣ A J 10 6 5 2
 ♠ K Q J 5   ┌─────────┐   ♠ 10 8 2
 ♥ K J 10 7 2   │   N   │   ♥ 6 5 3
 ♦ Q J 8 5   │ W   E │   ♦ A 9 3 2
 ♣ –   │   S   │   ♣ Q 9 3
                 └─────────┘
                   ♠ A 6 4
                   ♥ Q 8
                   ♦ K 10 6 4
                   ♣ K 8 7 4
</pre>

On a club lead declarer was five down undoubled.

The next hand was another tale of a missed opportunity:

Love All, IMPs, Dealer North

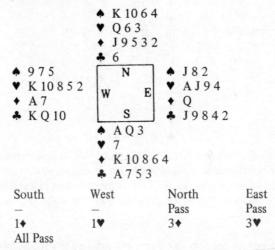

	♠ K 10 6 4	
	♥ Q 6 3	
	♦ J 9 5 3 2	
	♣ 6	
♠ 9 7 5		♠ J 8 2
♥ K 10 8 5 2		♥ A J 9 4
♦ A 7		♦ Q
♣ K Q 10		♣ J 9 8 4 2
	♠ A Q 3	
	♥ 7	
	♦ K 10 8 6 4	
	♣ A 7 5 3	

South	West	North	East
—	—	Pass	Pass
1♦	1♥	3♦	3♥
All Pass			

South defended as pessimistically as he had bid. On a diamond lead, declarer guessed the trumps correctly, drew three rounds, and played a club from dummy. South rose with the ace, and when the king dropped, continued with diamonds. 3♥ + 2 was a flattering result for East-West.

The bid of 3♦ was a pre-emptive raise, denying the values for an unassuming cue-bid of 2♥. South refrained from bidding over 3♥ for fear of driving the opponents to game in the higher ranking suit. A trial bid of 4♣ might have led to 4♥ doubled minus three, 5♦ made, or at worst 4♦ + 1.

Before drawing any conclusions about the technique of speculative doubles, let us consider a hand where it is virtually impossible to find the winning bid.

North-South Game, Dealer North

South	West	North	East
—	—	1♥	2♦
3♣	3♦	Pass	4♦
?			

South holds:

♠ A 10 3   ♥ 10 2   ♦ A   ♣ A 10 8 7 6 4 2

Do you double and take the money, or push on to 5♣ or more?

In fact the 'right' bid is pass, since 4♦ doubled was made, and 5♣ doubled would have gone for 500.

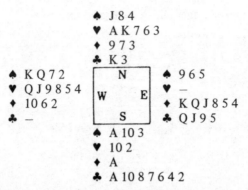

The point of quoting a hand such as this where any rational system of evaluation goes haywire is to show that in spite of two voids and a miraculous lie of the cards for East-West, the TNT is more or less as expected. The only extraordinary feature of the hand is the way the total number of tricks is shared out.

TNT is of course the starting point of analysis for any speculative double. First estimate your own trump length and guess at theirs. With nothing to act as a guide to their trump length, assume it is the same as yours. If there is a secondary fit, take that into consideration by adding one to the TNT. Then either the number of tricks your side can take is a good guide to the price of your sacrifice, or alternatively the number of tricks they claim to be able to take will be a clue to the price tag on your sacrifice.

Several factors relating to TNT theory affect the speculative double. Good features are values in the side suits, particularly aces, and side suits which are breaking unevenly for them. The worst features are a strong holding in your own trump suit, and a doubleton in their trump suit. A strong holding in your own trump suit is very likely to be cancelled out by their distributional features, and nine or ten points in one suit will take only one trick in defence, whereas a weak trump suit may mean a lower TNT and duplication of values. A doubleton in their trump suit means that trumps are breaking evenly for them, and declarer has much more manoeuvrability in the play of the hand.

There are three final questions:

1 How is the cake of TNT likely to be shared? Are the honour cards lying favourably for you or for them?

2 Why have they bid their final contract? Have they been hustled into possible error, or are they bidding it with the full intention of making it?

3 Is there a chance that declarer will lose trump control?

Let us look at some of the previous doubles in the light of these comments:

♠ 8 6	♥ A 10 9 5	♦ J 7 6 3	♣ A 6 5
—	—	1♣	Pass
1♥	4♦	4♥	?

Here they have been roughly handled by partner's bid of 4♦. The TNT is likely to be twenty, but could be lower in view of the values in both their suits. The ten and nine of trumps will certainly bring down the TNT, and declarer could easily lose trump control.

♠ 9 7 3	♥ A 9 4	♦ 7	♣ A J 10 6 5 2
—	—	Pass	Pass
1♦	3♣	Dble	3♠
Pass	4♠	?	

The true fit for your side is clubs which has not been investigated, but the side suit of diamonds is breaking badly. The aces are invaluable. There is a danger that partner has good clubs and that 5♣ is a make with 4♠ only one off. But the time has passed to bid clubs, it must be easier to take four tricks in defence, and to pass would be cowardly.

♠ A Q 3	♥ 7	♦ K 10 8 6 4	♣ A 7 5 3
—	—	Pass	Pass
1♦	1♥	3♦	3♥
?			

With such defence in the unbid suits it is a mistake to sell out to 3♥. The weak trump holding is no deterrent to bidding on and doubling 4♥. If partner has six diamonds and a doubleton heart and nothing to contribute to the defence, it is doubtful that he should stand the double of 4♥, and certainly he should not if you are playing a strong club system.

♠ A 10 3	♥ 10 2	♦ A	♣ A 10 8 7 6 4 2
—	—	1♥	2♦
3♣	3♦	Pass	4♦
?			

Of course there is no answer to this hand. The best defence against the opponents' high contracts bid on low point counts is repeated trump leads. To abandon any measure of trump control by cashing the ace of trumps is unattractive, and this consideration might lead South into bidding 5♣. It might only go one down if they do not break up the major suit squeeze.

Consider another problem:

North-South Game, IMPs

South	West	North	East
—	—	Pass	Pass
1♥	1♠	2♥	4♠
5♥	Pass	Pass	?

East holds:

♠ A 10 9 6 3   ♥ 4   ♦ A 8 5 4   ♣ Q 6 2

Pass, double, or 5♠?

For whom are the cards lying well? Why have they bid it? What about the hustle factor? Declarer is probably well stocked with minor suit honours, and these are lying well for him. At this vulnerability, and on this bidding, declarer is not sacrificing. He may have bid one more because he was not prepared to accept a small penalty in exchange for 620, but he is not going more than one off. There is no hustle factor, it is a simple everyday sequence, and South knows exactly what to expect in the dummy.

A double stands to gain an extra 100 points and lose 200. 5♠ reckons to concede 300 or 500 against a game which may not be making. Pass and defend, you may have done enough already.

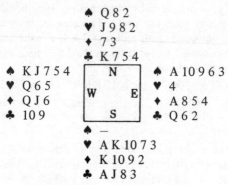

```
                    ♠ Q 8 2
                    ♥ J 9 8 2
                    ♦ 7 3
                    ♣ K 7 5 4
    ♠ K J 7 5 4    ┌─────────┐    ♠ A 10 9 6 3
    ♥ Q 6 5        │    N    │    ♥ 4
    ♦ Q J 6      W │         │ E  ♦ A 8 5 4
    ♣ 10 9         │    S    │    ♣ Q 6 2
                   └─────────┘
                    ♠ —
                    ♥ A K 10 7 3
                    ♦ K 10 9 2
                    ♣ A J 8 3
```

The final hand is again a problem in offensive/defensive evaluation:

South	West	North	East
—	Pass	Pass	1♥ (five cards)
3♦ (10-14)	3♥	?	

With neither side vulnerable, you, North, hold:

♠ A   ♥ 10 9 7 5   ♦ K 7 5 2   ♣ Q J 9 6

How would you rate, a) 4♦, b) 4♥ (unassuming cue-bid), c) 4♠ (slam try), d) 5♦?

a) 4♦ — offensively this is a magnificent hand with partner's shortage opposite your weakness. It is possible that there are two clubs and a heart to lose, but this is a very pessimistic view to take.

b) 4♥ — The purpose of an unassuming cue-bid is to tell partner that you are strong defensively, but the opponents are also listening. Partner has made a limit bid, and should not bid again if the opponents do bid 5♥. For whose benefit is the bid of 4♥?

c) 4♠ — A hand can be constructed where twelve tricks can be made in diamonds. But on more likely holdings, the bid of 4♠ prevents the opponents misjudging, either by doubling 5♦, or by bidding 5♥. Against 5♥ doubled it is essential to play a forcing game, a spade lead may snatch a quick ruff and allow the opponents off the hook very cheaply, for spades is their side suit.

d) 5♦ — They do not know you expect to make it, you would bid this way as a sacrifice. Let them guess.

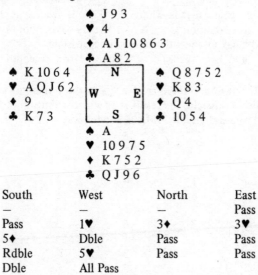

	♠ J 9 3		
	♥ 4		
	♦ A J 10 8 6 3		
	♣ A 8 2		

♠ K 10 6 4	N	♠ Q 8 7 5 2
♥ A Q J 6 2	W　E	♥ K 8 3
♦ 9		♦ Q 4
♣ K 7 3	S	♣ 10 5 4

	♠ A
	♥ 10 9 7 5
	♦ K 7 5 2
	♣ Q J 9 6

South	West	North	East
—	—	—	Pass
Pass	1♥	3♦	3♥
5♦	Dble	Pass	Pass
Rdble	5♥	Pass	Pass
Dble	All Pass		

Presumably West ran from the redouble of 5♦ because he had no faith in his own double. In that sense his judgment was correct.

He refused the force in diamonds and threw a club, but was then forced in clubs. After two rounds of trumps, he played a spade to the queen, and eventually emerged with six tricks for −900.

Admittedly opponents on this hand have neither bid nor played well. But that is what doubling is all about, smelling out an indiscretion, and exacting the full penalty.

Chapter 26
Monster TNT

Potential double game swings where the TNT is twenty or twenty-one are common. Far less common is a TNT of twenty-two or more where game in one room and slam in the other room is a possibility. This is the realm of monster TNT, and here the rule of combined trump length tends to break down.

If both sides have an eleven-card fit, and the remaining cards are distributed as evenly as possible, the result is a total distribution of 11-7-6-2 which can be divided round the table in the following way:

		5		
		1		
		3		
1		4		1
6				5
3				4
3		6		3
		1		
		3		
		3		

With these suit patterns the TNT is almost certain to be eighteen, and there is no way that it can be higher than twenty. If the high cards are evenly shared, leading to a competitive auction, whoever buys the final contract will be disappointed. If the preponderance of high cards lie in one direction, a slam will probably fail on duplication.

Complete duplication of distributional features like this is extremely infrequent. Set out:

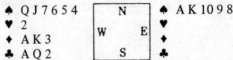

and it is easy to see that the deal would have to be completed many, many, times before East had a singleton heart and North and South each had a singleton spade and even then the minor suits probably would not break evenly. Nonetheless the point is made that two eleven-card fits do not necessarily entail a high TNT. With a TNT of eighteen there may be no game on for either side.

The overwhelming consideration in monster TNT is voids. To have a TNT of twenty-six, a double grand slam, there must be at least four voids in the deal because no ace is cashable in defence. Similarly a TNT of twenty-five entails three voids, a TNT of twenty-four entails two voids, and there must be at least one void for a TNT of twenty-three. Although theoretically a genuine TNT of twenty-two with no misdefence can exist without a void, in practice it seldom does. The Duke of Cumberland whist hand is the classical example of monster TNT, showing the importance of voids and the comparative unimportance of trump length.

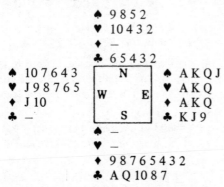

```
                    ♠ 9 8 5 2
                    ♥ 10 4 3 2
                    ♦ —
                    ♣ 6 5 4 3 2
   ♠ 10 7 6 4 3      ┌─────────┐      ♠ A K Q J
   ♥ J 9 8 7 6 5     │    N    │      ♥ A K Q
   ♦ J 10            │ W     E │      ♦ A K Q
   ♣ —               │    S    │      ♣ K J 9
                     └─────────┘
                    ♠ —
                    ♥ —
                    ♦ 9 8 7 6 5 4 3 2
                    ♣ A Q 10 8 7
```

A TNT of twenty-six on a combined trump length of nineteen.

Roughly one thirteen-card hand in twenty contains a void. But because flat hands tend to co-exist and so do voids, it would be a mistake to conclude that one deal in five has a void. Any player knows that voids are not that frequent; many players, however, would be surprised to know that with proper shuffling about one deal in nine contains a void. Nearly half the deals which have a void also contain a second or even third void. The practical fact that emerges is that if you hold a void it is almost an even money shot that someone else has a void on the same deal.

A study of freak deals shows than one unusual hand pattern almost inevitably entails others. This is not surprising. What is more surprising is that no matter how outlandish the deal there is nearly always one hand out of the four whose pattern is quite ordinary. G.C.H. Fox's Book of Bridge is a collection of interesting hands and as such it contains more than a normal percentage of unusual hands. The longest suit is an eleven-carder and the distribution is 11-0-1-1. Needless to say there are two other voids lurking around the table, but the fourth hand is 4-4-3-2. If you are sitting looking at a boring everyday hand and suddenly the bidding goes mad, do not assume that your companions have taken leave of their senses, yours is the odd usual hand. By all means double if you hold K-Q-x or Q-J-x in their trump suit, but do not double just because you have a flat hand.

The value of a void varies according to where it is held. In the sequence:

1♣	1♠	2♦	4♠
Pass	Pass	?	

opener's pass is not forcing but any pretext is good enough for responder to find another bid. Which is the best responding hand?

♠ —   ♥ J 10 7   ♦ A Q J 9 7 3 2   ♣ J 10 4

or

♠ J 10 7   ♥ —   ♦ A Q J 9 7 3 2   ♣ J 10 4

or

♠ J 10 7   ♥ J 10 4   ♦ A Q J 9 7 3 2   ♣ —

It is easy to see that either the void in the opponent's suit or the void in the unbid suit could mean that six of a minor is a make. Offensively and defensively the void in partner's suit is a totally useless feature; and as a general rule it always will be.

Either of the hands with a void in the major has monster potential. In fact it was the second hand which occurred in a pairs contest, and at one table the bidding was:

South	West	North	East
—	—	1♣	1♠
2♦	4♠	Pass (i)	Pass
4NT (ii)	5♦ (iii)	5♠ (iv)	Dble (v)
6♦ (vi)	6♠ (vii)	Dble (viii)	Pass
Pass (ix)	Pass		

The contract was made on the uninspired defence of jack and another club. The full deal was:

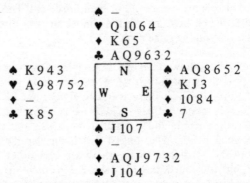

As can be imagined the travelling score sheet at the end of the evening bore considerable resemblance to a Rolls Royce profit and loss sheet.

The players' comments on their own bids were interesting:

(i)   Pass — Forcing, certainly at pairs

(ii)   4NT — Both minors

(iii) 5♦ — Lead diamonds against a club slam partner

(iv) 5♠ — A void, you choose the minor

(v)   Dble — No-one questioned the bid and no explanation was volunteered. Why should he worry, he had just made a doubled slam. Perhaps he thought the world had gone mad because he had an everyday hand.

(vi) 6♦ — Guessed what the bid of 5♦ meant

(vii) 6♠ — Did not like the prospect of defending 6♦ nearly as much as defending 6♣.

(viii) Dble — 'I couldn't believe that it could possibly make'.

(ix)   Pass — 'I assumed that you could beat it? If you had passed I would have bid 7♦, and it can't be touched'.

At pairs a monster TNT such as this is no more important than an overtrick or an undertrick in a part-score, but imagine what a deal like this could do to a close team of four match.

This deal contains an ingredient common to many monster hands, misdefence. Defenders should sort out their length signals to prevent contracts like this getting through, and it does not require a World Champion in the South seat to find the diamond switch which ensures killing dummy's heart suit. But when there is a double fit and one or more voids lying in ambush, not even a World Champion is going to find the right blind opening lead all the time. For this reason monster TNT occurs more frequently in practice than theoretically it should against perfect defence.

In the realm of monster TNT there are three precepts:

a)   Believe the opponents

b)   Play the hand

c)   No way of bidding the hand is correct. There is only one successful way, and that is the way that allows you to play the hand.

a) Believe the opponents

In a long session of short deck Poker peculiar things happen. If three players decline the opportunity of changing cards and a fourth player draws cards and raises the limit something rather odd and rather expensive is about to take place. The remaining three players may each have their own ideas on the subject. The bet is so outrageous that it must be genuine; the bet is so outrageous that it must be a bluff; the bet should be called to keep him honest. The winning player is the player who quietly puts his chips in the middle and lets the others sort it out.

Not only the ethics, but also the mathematics of Bridge are totally different to those of Poker. If you and your partner are having a nice little part-score sequence when some lunatic opponent comes leaping in at the five or six level, what should you do? Many players would double him for his cheek. That is the very last thing you should do. Unless you know for certain that he is bluffing or sacrificing, either pass and let partner share the decision or outbid him. At the end of the chapter on believing the opponents there was a sequence: 1♠ - Pass - 2♦ - 6♣. Opener held:

♠ A K J 10 4   ♥ J 8 3   ♦ A 7 4 2   ♣ 6

West says he can make twelve tricks. Improbable, but so is the bid and he has just made it. Where might these tricks come from? Obviously clubs and hearts. If he has twelve tricks and you do not believe him it will be very expensive. At Poker perhaps you lose a sizeable pot which you could have won for believing the opponents. On this hand of Bridge, it costs the price of 6♦ doubled, whatever that may be.

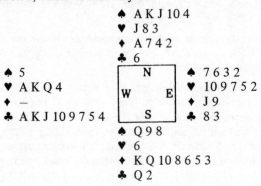

b) Play the hand

The deal that follows comes from a Swiss Teams Competition of seven board matches:

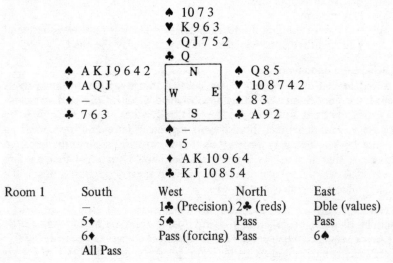

Room 1	South	West	North	East
	—	1♣ (Precision)	2♣ (reds)	Dble (values)
	5♦	5♠	Pass	Pass
	6♦	Pass (forcing)	Pass	6♠
	All Pass			

Room 2	South	West	North	East
	–	2♣ (Benj)	Pass	2♥
	Pass	2♠	Pass	2NT
	Pass	3♠	Pass	4♠
	4NT	5♠	6♦	Dble
	All Pass			

Both West and South know that the hand is a potential freak. In Room 1 West was Bob Rowlands, securing the contract for his side; in Room 2 Dimmie Fleming as South won the contract for her side. Looking at the North-South, and then at the East-West cards you do not want to be in a slam in either direction. But that is not what the game is all about. The chief objective is to prevent the opponents from playing a potential freak. If either slam makes, perhaps on a misdefence, the match is won; if neither makes, the opponents have a few measley IMPs which they could lose on the next part-score hand.

As a further illustration of the vital necessity of playing the hand, cover up the West and South cards and imagine defending 6♦ from the East seat, as might have happened in Room 1. On the probably lead of the ace of spades declarer ruffs and leads a club to the queen. There is no reason to suppose that the actual East would have done anything else except win and switch to a heart, but he certainly would not have enjoyed the post mortem if he had played back any of his other three suits.

Incidentally, as can be seen from the diagram, 6♠ is unbeatable on any defence, and there is the match won.

c) It does not matter how you bid as long as you win the auction

♠ K 10 7 6 4 3   ♥ –   ♦ A 9 7 5 4   ♣ 8 2

This is another potential monster TNT since the bidding starts: 1♥ - 2♦ - 3♥ - ? Vulnerability on this type of exercise is immaterial, all you know is that the piece of paper thrust under your nose originates from a team of four match. There is no correct bid on a hand of this type. Pass, 3♠, 3NT, 4♦, 5♦, or 6♦ all have something to commend them. What is important is not what you bid now, but what happens on the second and third rounds. In principle it is unwise to introduce a second suit into the auction if you are outgunned, or if the information will be more valuable to the opponents than to partner. But when you say that you will string along with the bid that was made at the table, you find that you have bid 3♠. The second round of betting is:

1♥	2♦	3♥	3♠
4♥	4♠	5♥	?

You cannot refrain from commenting that 5♥ is either another freak or an ill disciplined bid by a limited hand in front of an unlimited partner, but you are reminded that that is not the point, it is your bid. Well of course you only introduced the spades in order to outrank the enemy at the same level, so you bid 5♠. Whereupon you are informed that you have taken the wrong decision. Partner held:

♠ A 8   ♥ A 4   ♦ K Q J 8 2   ♣ 10 6 5 4

and wanted to double 5♥ which was not making. Bully for partner, presumably he would also have liked to double 5♥ on:

♠ A 8   ♥ 6 4   ♦ K Q J 8 2   ♣ A 6 5 4

with a grand slam rigid our way, and even on the actual hand 6♦ is only beaten on a club lead which may well be difficult to find.

Apparently the bid of 5♠ came in for a lot of criticism at the table. This criticism must have been based entirely on hindsight. Any player who suppresses this type of trump support and then allows the opponents to play in 5♥ doubled has missed his vocation. He should have been a Kami Kaze pilot.

To return to the previous hand, consider South's problem in Room 1 after: 1♣ - 2♣ - Dble - ?

♠ –   ♥ 5   ♦ A K 10 9 6 4   ♣ K J 10 8 5 4

5♦ followed by 6♦ is not the best ploy, but not for the reason suggested at the time, that such bidding is contrary to the principles of pre-emption.

Let us digress to formulate these principles of pre-emption with the help of a hand from a different match in the same competition:

North-South Game, Dealer West

```
                    ♠ 8 7
                    ♥ Q 9 5 4 3
                    ♦ 6 2
                    ♣ A 9 3 2
  ♠ A Q 10 4 3    ┌─────────┐    ♠ 9 5
  ♥ 7 6           │    N    │    ♥ 10
  ♦ 5             │ W     E │    ♦ A K Q J 10 9 7 3
  ♣ Q J 10 8 7    │    S    │    ♣ 6 4
                  └─────────┘
                    ♠ K J 6 2
                    ♥ A K J 8 2
                    ♦ 8 4
                    ♣ K 5
```

South	West	North	East
–	Pass	Pass	3NT
Dble	Pass	Pass	4♦
Pass	Pass	4♥	5♦
Dble	All Pass		

Although East-West were satisfied with their result, their bidding was really terrible. A pre-emptive bid should describe a hand within limits, and that player should pass thereafter, leaving any further action to his partner who is in command because he knows the combined resources. East must decide whether to open 3NT or 5♦, and having done so, abide by his partner's decision. West's pass of 3NT doubled should mean that he is prepared to play there. 4♠ clearly means that East does not trust his partner. 5♦ in front of partner is grotesque. When East originally picks up his hand all he knows is that the opponents can make something ranging between a partscore and a grand slam in one of three suits. That is also all they know, yet they have been given six bids to find out what they need to know. Such bidding ought not to exist outside a beginners' class-room.

On the hand against Bob Rowlands these principles do not apply. You are not making a descriptive bid with the intention of adopting a subordinate role and letting partner take the final decision, in fact you in the happy position of knowing more about the hand than anyone else, for what that is worth. Neither are you trying to bounce the opponents out of an unknown fit, they have spades and they are going to bid them, for Bob has never been known not to bid them.

Against a less experienced player it might be helpful to find a few fatuities to while away the initial rounds of the auction. But if the opponent has been around for some time he is not going to take much notice of pass, redouble, or 2NT when the final bid in diamonds comes up.

Before considering how to bid, let us define the objectives. First, to play in 5♦, preferably doubled; second, to play in 6♦; third and last, to defend against 6♠ on the assumption that clubs, diamonds and hearts will between them produce two defensive tricks.

On the almost certain premise that spades are going to be bid and supported, there are six ways of developing the auction, ignoring joke bids other than diamonds: an immediate 6♦; 5♦ followed by 6♦ if necessary; 4♦. 5♦, 6♦; 3♦, 4♦, 6♦; 2♦, 4♦, 5♦, 6♦; 2♦, Pass, 5♦, 6♦.

The immediate 6♦ is the poorest investment. If opener's hand is weak offensively he will probably double, but if that is the case he might have snapped at 5♦ if the hook had been appetisingly presented. If he is strong offensively he will work out how much he is getting from 6♦ doubled, and if he comes up with the answer 100 and goes on to work out that 6♠ is worth 1430, he will bid 6♠ on any odds better than 10-1 against.

The trouble with 5♦, 6♦ is that what actually happened is all too probable.

Any of the remaining four sequences could win the jackpot according to the state of the opponents' digestion and their opinion of your abilities. The only 'correct' way to bid is the way that buys the contract. As far as the principles of pre-emption are concerned, they have to be bent to the overriding principle of monster TNT. Play the hand unless partner says not to, and even then think twice before taking his advice.

An idea mentioned above is worth pursuing: the odds needed to bid a slam in competition. Players accustomed to bidding a small slam on a finesse or better are not always fully aware that the situation is dramatically changed when the opponents are threatening to win the contract.

Consider the auction: 1♥ - 4♠ - 5♥ - 5♠. The opening side will not automatically hold the balance of strength, but will nearly always wish to double or bid on. Which is correct, double or 6♥? That is an awkward question which is not necessarily answered more easily by looking at one of the hands. Opener's assets and his partner's measured in terms of trumps, playing strength, and controls will be divided in such a way that neither player will be able to bid the slam with any degree of confidence. It is a nasty guessing game, but at least it is a mathematical guessing game where there is a glib answer: double at pairs, bid 6♥ at teams. The justification is as follows: At match-pointed pairs, or at point-a-board scoring, the object is to be right more often than not, regardless of how much it costs on the few occasions when one is wrong. 5♠ will usually fail, 6♥ will usually fail, therefore either opener or responder should close his eyes and double 5♠ unless he can see some good reason for doing otherwise.

At aggregate, rubber bridge, or 1MPS, neither 5♠ nor 6♥ would stand any better chance of making, but the mathematics of the scoring is vastly different. Either opener or responder must do a little sum, estimate what 5♠ doubled is going to be worth, and compare that to the value of a possible slam. If 5♠ doubled is going to yield 100/300 (it is unlikely to produce more), and the slam is vulnerable, 1430, it can be seen that a slam requiring two finesses is a very good slam to bid. Furthermore if the slam is bid smoothly, it does not have to be made, at least not until the opponents have solved their problems, they will not be happy to defend and may well pay an extra 200 for a phantom sacrifice.

A hand from a team of four match provides a good illustration of these ideas:

East-West Game. IMPs. Dealer East

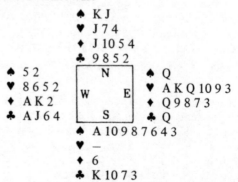

In both rooms the bidding started: 1♥ - 4♠ - 5♥, but thereafter the paths diverged. One North bid an aggressive 5♠ which was passed to West who.

doubled for +100. The other North, not wishing to be faced with the dilemma of an expensive phantom sacrifice against 6♥, made the technically correct bid of pass, and 5♥ was made with an overtrick for a loss of 11 IMPs. In the other room where 5♠ doubled was taken one off, if North-South fail to sacrifice against 6♥, there is a turnover of 24 IMPs.

Note, of course, that neither East nor West is well placed to bid the lay-down slam. If it is accepted that the slam must be bid at this scoring and vulnerability, East is the man to do it, his partner cannot know that four or five small trumps, the two minor aces and the jack of diamonds will give an adequate play for twelve tricks, and if his partner is not as good as this the defence to 5♠ will not be comfortable.

Slams in competition are the last word in Monster TNT. They don't have to be made, they just have to be bid. From time to time one will slip through as if by accident, and that is enough.

Chapter 27
The Human Factor

The quickest way for a sponsor to lose money would be to stage a par contest. With carefully prepared hands where marks are allotted for expertise in bidding and play, the result would be a ranking list of technical merit. Such an event would be doomed to failure. Bridge players do not want the results they deserve. They want their bad contracts and flights of fancy to succeed sometimes. They want the chance to beat a better team with a little luck and a few hands to suit their methods. There is more to bridge than technical expertise; confidence, morale, the human element. Remove that, and there might be more chess players, but there would be a lot less bridge players.

Sam and Fred were lying third in a big pairs contest after the first of two sessions, and feeling pretty keen.

On the first board of the second session, Sam as dealer, picked up:

♠ J 2   ♥ K 3   ♦ K 7 6 4   ♣ A 10 9 6 3

Vulnerable against not, he decided that values such as these were quite sufficient to open the bidding when things were going well, and he fully intended to make sure things did go well. The bidding became rather lively, and the opponents finished in a very speculative contract of 4♥. There was no defence, and it was clear that game was not going to be bid at the other tables.

A few boards later Fred felt that:

♠ A Q 10 8 3   ♥ J 3   ♦ 7 4   ♣ J 10 8 6

constituted a compulsory Multi. Next hand came in with 2NT, and Sam raised to 4♦ on:

♠ J 9 7 2   ♥ K 9 8 4   ♦ Q J 10 3   ♣ 9

The bid of 4♠ from Fred presented no problem to his left hand opponent who knew exactly what to do to ten trick contracts when he held an eighteen count. Minus three hundred caused no undue anxiety to our heroes. Fred's multis seldom went for less. What was disturbing, however, was the score sheet, which revealed games going down by the opponents.

Sam and Fred continued on their way assuring each other that there was no need to press, the opponents looked dumb and would soon start chucking. The opponents did not chuck nearly as much as Sam and Fred felt entitled to expect.

It was Sam's firm belief that you did not win at Pairs by allowing the opponents to play the hands. He appreciated the necessity of defending 40 per cent of the time, but didn't like doing it, and felt the opponents' fair share was nearer 30 per cent.

Halfway through the session even the most optimistic assessment could not score the card at more than half a top above average. Sam picked up:

♠ A 9 5 3 2   ♥ 9 2   ♦ Q 5 2   ♣ Q 6 2

and listened to: 1♦ - 1♥ - Pass - ? at love all. Being accustomed to introducing the spade suit with less points and fewer spades, he made a routine bid of 1♠. 2♦ - Pass - Pass back to Sam. Not a technical problem. No way of guessing how good the contract of 2♦ might be. Just a gut reaction. Sam's gut told him to bid 2♥. But instead of bidding it quickly and confidently he thought about it and decided he ought not to. For Sam this was an uncharacteristic well-disciplined decision. Unfortunately the full hand was:

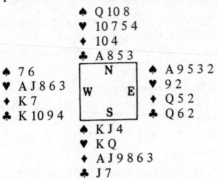

2♦ was just made. Some pairs had been making 2♥, once with an overtrick. Sam knew that he had chucked. If there were eight or nine tricks to be had on the deal, Fred would certainly have found them. Sam was rattled, and he missed an overtrick on the next board.

A few boards later, again at love all, Sam's right hand opponent opened a mini and Sam was looking at:

♠ A 9 3   ♥ A 10 8 7 5 3 2   ♦ 4   ♣ J 3

In the normal course of events Sam would have bid some large number of hearts and passed the problem to someone else. But Sam was not feeling too confident at this stage, and settled for a peaceful 2♥. The bidding proceeded:

1NT	2♥	3♣	3♥
3♠	4♥	4♠	Pass
Pass	?		

Sam looked at his two aces and a singleton, and decided to defend. He led his singleton, and obtained a ruff, but to no avail.

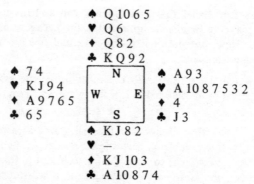

♠ Q 10 6 5
♥ Q 6
♦ Q 8 2
♣ K Q 9 2

♠ 7 4
♥ K J 9 4
♦ A 9 7 6 5
♣ 6 5

♠ A 9 3
♥ A 10 8 7 5 3 2
♦ 4
♣ J 3

♠ K J 8 2
♥ —
♦ K J 10 3
♣ A 10 8 7 4

South said he would have bid 5♠.

On the next round the opponents bid a grand slam in no-trumps which made on a 3-3 break, and that was the end of Fred and Sam.

On the way to the bar, they met John and Harry, their team-mates for the Swiss Teams. John asked how it had gone, disgustedly Fred retorted that they had run out of luck. 'It wasn't luck that we ran out of,' said Sam, 'it was morale!'

The Swiss Teams in the evening started well. John had an interesting decision in the second seven board match. At game all Harry dealt and opened 1♦. John held:

♠ A K Q J 3   ♥ 9 3   ♦ A 10   ♣ A Q 9 4

The bidding proceeded:

1♦	2♠
3♦	4♦
4♥	5NT
7♦	?

4♥ guaranteed the ace, 5NT was a grand slam force, and 7♦ showed two top honours.

Partner was marked with at least king, queen to five diamonds, the ace of hearts, and sufficient additional values to make up an opening bid. Could 7♦ be better than 7NT? Only by ruffing out the king of clubs, highly improbable; or with a heart ruff in dummy, impossible. Could 7♠ be better than 7♦? Yes, if partner had:

♠ x x   ♥ A x x   ♦ K Q x x x   ♣ K x x

The thirteenth trick would come from ruffing out the long diamond. If partner did not like 7♠, he knew that the controls were there, and he could convert to 7NT. It had to be right to bid 7♠.

A sound imaginative analysis such as one would expect since John was an expert of considerable experience and reputation. It would be unlucky to lose points on the deal.

Before revealing Harry's hand, let's sketch in the human factor. In comparison to John, Harry was inexperienced. During the afternoon John had lost no opportunity to point out Harry's shortcomings. To say that Harry was demoralised would have been a gross understatement. At first he had been unable to believe that he was quite such a cretin as John seemed to think he was. In the later stages of the session he had been deliberating between running amok with an axe and disappearing unobtrusively to open up a vein. As for getting through the evening session, Harry had decided to anaesthetise himself with as many pints of beer as he could, and stay as far as possible out of the range of his partner's tongue.

From Harry's point of view the contract of 7♠ held various attractions. He had not yet done anything wrong in the auction, as far as he could see. Though he had learnt in the course of the afternoon that this did not necessarily confer immunity, it was nevertheless a distinct advantage not to have made any bids which made him feel nervous. A more obvious advantage of 7♠ was that there was no risk of him misplaying it since he would be dummy. Finally, and perhaps most important, 7♠ would enable him to replenish his glass.

Later Harry was forced to do some fast thinking, and was heard to mutter something about a void club. At the time if anyone had suggested that he should consider converting John's bid of 7♠ to 7NT, it is certain that he would have greeted the idea with the same enthusiasm as if someone had suggested unarmed combat with the lions in the arena. As it was he was happy to put his hand down:

♠ 7   ♥ A Q   ♦ K Q J 9 7 6 5   ♣ 10 8 2

and scuttle off to the bar.

He timed his exit well. John was giving no outward signs of displeasure. A few minutes later Harry returned with a brimming glass, blissfully unaware of the 5-2 break which had been beyond the competence of even John to handle.

Index